Banking: A Very Short Introduction

VERY SHORT INTRODUCTIONS are for anyone wanting a stimulating and accessible way into a new subject. They are written by experts, and have been translated into more than 45 different languages.

The series began in 1995, and now covers a wide variety of topics in every discipline. The VSI library now contains over 500 volumes—a Very Short Introduction to everything from Psychology and Philosophy of Science to American History and Relativity—and continues to grow in every subject area.

Titles in the series include the following:

ACCOUNTING Christopher Nobes
ADOLESCENCE Peter K. Smith
ADVERTISING Winston Fletcher
AFRICAN AMERICAN RELIGION
    Eddie S. Glaude Jr
AFRICAN HISTORY John Parker and
    Richard Rathbone
AFRICAN RELIGIONS
    Jacob K. Olupona
AGEING Nancy A. Pachana
AGNOSTICISM Robin Le Poidevin
AGRICULTURE Paul Brassley and
    Richard Soffe
ALEXANDER THE GREAT
    Hugh Bowden
ALGEBRA Peter M. Higgins
AMERICAN HISTORY Paul S. Boyer
AMERICAN IMMIGRATION
    David A. Gerber
AMERICAN LEGAL HISTORY
    G. Edward White
AMERICAN POLITICAL
    HISTORY Donald Critchlow
AMERICAN POLITICAL PARTIES
    AND ELECTIONS L. Sandy Maisel
AMERICAN POLITICS
    Richard M. Valelly
THE AMERICAN
    PRESIDENCY Charles O. Jones
THE AMERICAN REVOLUTION
    Robert J. Allison
AMERICAN SLAVERY
    Heather Andrea Williams
THE AMERICAN WEST Stephen Aron

AMERICAN WOMEN'S HISTORY
    Susan Ware
ANAESTHESIA Aidan O'Donnell
ANARCHISM Colin Ward
ANCIENT ASSYRIA Karen Radner
ANCIENT EGYPT Ian Shaw
ANCIENT EGYPTIAN ART AND
    ARCHITECTURE Christina Riggs
ANCIENT GREECE Paul Cartledge
THE ANCIENT NEAR EAST
    Amanda H. Podany
ANCIENT PHILOSOPHY Julia Annas
ANCIENT WARFARE Harry Sidebottom
ANGELS David Albert Jones
ANGLICANISM Mark Chapman
THE ANGLO-SAXON AGE
    John Blair
ANIMAL BEHAVIOUR
    Tristram D. Wyatt
THE ANIMAL KINGDOM
    Peter Holland
ANIMAL RIGHTS David DeGrazia
THE ANTARCTIC Klaus Dodds
ANTISEMITISM Steven Beller
ANXIETY Daniel Freeman and
    Jason Freeman
THE APOCRYPHAL GOSPELS
    Paul Foster
ARCHAEOLOGY Paul Bahn
ARCHITECTURE Andrew Ballantyne
ARISTOCRACY William Doyle
ARISTOTLE Jonathan Barnes
ART HISTORY Dana Arnold
ART THEORY Cynthia Freeland

John Goddard and
John O. S. Wilson

BANKING

A Very Short Introduction

OXFORD
UNIVERSITY PRESS

OXFORD

UNIVERSITY PRESS

Great Clarendon Street, Oxford, OX2 6DP,
United Kingdom

Oxford University Press is a department of the University of Oxford.
It furthers the University's objective of excellence in research, scholarship,
and education by publishing worldwide. Oxford is a registered trade mark of
Oxford University Press in the UK and in certain other countries

© John Goddard and John O. S. Wilson 2016

The moral rights of the authors have been asserted

First edition published in 2016

Published in the United States of America by Oxford University Press
198 Madison Avenue, New York, NY 10016, United States of America

British Library Cataloguing in Publication Data
Data available

Library of Congress Control Number: 2016946828

ISBN 978-0-19-968892-0

Printed and bound by
CPI Group (UK) Ltd, Croydon, CR0 4YY

For Sarah, Aimée, Thomas, and
Chris   John Goddard
For Alison, Kathryn, Elizabeth, and
Jean   John O. S. Wilson

Contents

Acknowledgements

We would like to thank Andrea Keegan and Jenny Nugee at
Oxford University Press for commissioning and managing the
development of this volume through to completion. We wish to
thank three anonymous reviewers for helpful comments and
suggestions that have greatly improved the text. Finally, we would
like to thank our families for their patience and support
throughout the process of writing this volume.

List of illustrations

List of tables

Chapter 1
Origins and function of banking

A bank is an institution that accepts deposits from savers, extends loans to borrowers, and provides a range of other financial services to its customers. Banks are a central part of the modern financial system. Banks play a key role in organizing the flows of funds between savers and borrowers, including households, companies, and the government. In recent decades advances in information technology have delivered major changes in the quality and range of banking services, and have generated cost savings for banks. Customers in many countries use electronic distribution channels, such as automated teller machines, telephone and mobile banking, and internet banking, to gain access to banking services, in preference to visiting traditional high-street branches. Innovations in payments have led to a shift away from cash and cheques to faster and more convenient electronic payment systems, such as credit and debit cards, and contactless payment technologies, in some cases linked directly to customer bank accounts. Those parts of society unable to access the new distribution channels, however, have been denied many of the benefits of technological progress. Less visible to the banking public has been the rise of the 'shadow banking' system, comprising financial institutions that offer similar services to banks, but operate without banking licenses and largely beyond the scope of regulation.

The recent history of banking has witnessed the inexorable growth of large banking organizations, the biggest of which now span the globe. Much of the growth of the largest banks has been fuelled by the acquisition of competitors, sometimes at the height of banking or financial crises when banks in financial difficulty have been bailed out or rescued. Even the largest banks are inherently fragile and vulnerable to the possibility of collapse. A bank's depositors expect the bank will always be willing and able to cash their deposits quickly; but when a bank grants a loan to a borrower, the funds tied up in the loan may not be accessible to the bank for many years, until the loan is due for repayment. Provided all of the bank's depositors do not demand to withdraw their deposits simultaneously, the bank should be able to meet its commitments to depositors, and remain solvent. However, banks are vulnerable to a possible loss of depositor confidence. If all depositors seek to withdraw their funds simultaneously, the bank may soon run out of the cash it needs to repay them.

Until 2007, many commentators would have agreed that modern, technologically sophisticated banks, operating within a system of light-touch regulation, would always be able to provide plentiful finance for borrowers seeking to invest. The global financial crisis of 2007–9 was a rude awakening, and has led to a fundamental reappraisal of this view. During the crisis many banks suffered huge losses, some went out of business, and others required large taxpayer-funded bailouts to avoid collapse. As many economies entered recession, governments encountered large public spending deficits and mounting public debt. The global financial crisis was followed by a sovereign debt crisis, affecting countries such as Greece, Ireland, Portugal, and Spain. Central banks around the world have implemented unconventional monetary policies in an attempt to boost economic activity. New laws have been passed, and new rules imposed, to constrain the freedom of banks to undertake risky lending. New supervisory frameworks have been developed to monitor not only the risk of individual banks, but also the stability of the entire financial system.

Society benefits when the banking system operates efficiently and borrowers and depositors are able to realize their aims. Economic growth and development are hindered if promising investment opportunities remain unexploited because entrepreneurs are unable to borrow the funds they need to exploit these opportunities. A poorly performing or underdeveloped financial system can present an obstacle to growth and prosperity, if loans are granted for unproductive purposes dictated by family connections, political influence, or cronyism.

The key role of banks in the financial system and the vulnerability of banks to sudden collapse, owing to a loss of confidence on the part of depositors or other providers of funding, are recurring themes throughout this Very Short Introduction. This book highlights the financial services banks provide, the risks they face, and the role of the central bank. The book describes the main events of the global financial crisis and the sovereign debt crisis, and investigates the ways in which the banks themselves, industry supervisors and regulators, central banks, governments, and international agencies have adapted to the harsh lessons learned from the upheavals of the past decade.

A short history of banking

The earliest-known money-lending activities have been identified in historical civilizations and societies including Assyria, Babylon, ancient Greece, and the Roman Empire. Modern-day banking can be traced back to medieval and early Renaissance Italy, where privately-owned merchant banks were established to finance trade and channel private savings into government borrowing or other forms of public use. Private banks were typically constituted as partnerships, owned and managed by a family or some other group of individuals, and operating without the explicit sanction of government. Amsterdam became a leading financial and banking centre at the height of the Dutch Republic during the

17th century; succeeded by London during the 18th century, partly as a consequence of the growth in demand for banking services fuelled by the Industrial Revolution and the expansion of the British Empire. The first shareholder-owned bank in England was the Bank of England, founded in 1694 primarily to act as a vehicle for government borrowing to finance war with France. Despite its important role in raising public finance, the Bank of England did not assume its modern-day position as the government's bank until the 20th century.

Acceptance of the principle that banks could be owned by large pools of shareholders was key to the evolution of modern commercial banks. Shareholder-owned banks could grow much larger than private banks by issuing or accumulating shareholder capital. The shareholder bank's lifetime was indefinite, not contingent on the lives and deaths of individual partners. The Bank of England was originally incorporated with unlimited shareholder liability, meaning that in the event of failure shareholders would not only lose the capital they had invested, but were also liable for their share of any debts the bank had incurred. The same applied to private banks constituted as partnerships. Unlimited liability was seen as essential, because banks had powers to issue banknotes, and might do so recklessly unless their shareholders were ultimately liable when the holders of banknotes demanded redemption.

In England the introduction of shareholder banks was inhibited by the prohibition, until the early 19th century, of the issue of banknotes by banks with more than six partners. During the 18th century, the population of small private banks had increased; but many had insufficient resources to withstand financial shocks. Legislation passed in 1826 granted banknote-issuing powers to private banks with more than six partners headquartered outside a 65-mile radius of London. In 1844 the issue of banknotes was tied to gold reserves, paving the way for the Bank of England eventually to become the sole note-issuing bank. The inscription

4

that appears on all English banknotes 'I promise to pay the bearer on demand the sum of…', signed by the Chief Cashier on behalf of the Governor of the Bank of England, dates historically from the time when the Bank of England accepted a liability to convert any banknote into gold on request. The gold standard was abandoned by Britain at the start of the First World War, reintroduced in 1925 but abandoned again, permanently, in 1931.

The year 1844 also saw the establishment of a banking code, comprising detailed regulations on governance, management, and financial reporting. With a framework now in place for the charter and regulation of banks, the case for shareholder banks to be granted limited liability status and brought under the wings of general joint stock company law gained traction. Limited liability status was permitted in legislation passed during the 1850s, eliminating a major constraint on the growth of individual banks. Subsequently a trend towards the consolidation of shareholder and privately-owned banks through merger and acquisition progressed steadily, resulting in the emergence of several large commercial banks with nationwide office networks. By 1920 the 'big five', Westminster, National Provincial, Barclays, Lloyds, and Midland, accounted for around 80 per cent of all bank deposits in England and Wales. These five banks continued to dominate throughout the Great Depression of the 1930s and the Second World War. The high-street branch networks of the 'big five' and others proliferated during the 1950s and 1960s. The more recent evolution of the UK's major high-street banks is traced in Figure 1.

The most important mutually-owned depository institutions in the UK were the building societies, which first emerged in the late 18th century, using members' subscriptions to finance the construction of houses for members. The original building societies, which ceased trading when all members had acquired houses, were superseded during the 19th century by permanent building societies, which continued to trade on a rolling basis by

Banking

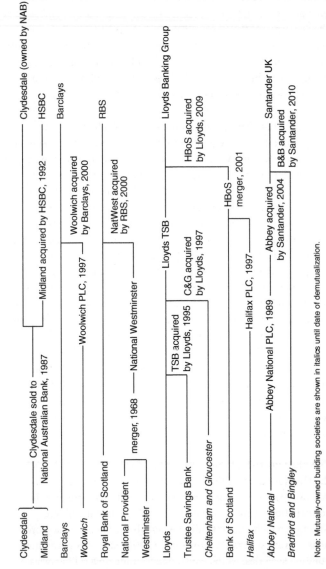

Note: Mutually-owned building societies are shown in italics until date of demutualization.

1. Evolution of UK retail banks.

acquiring new members. In the 1980s legislation was passed allowing building societies to demutualize, and acquire the status of limited companies like other commercial banks. Several of the larger building societies did so; others disappeared through acquisition or nationalization. Around forty independent UK building societies survived into the mid-2010s.

Meanwhile the Bank of England continued its evolution towards its current status as the government's bank. The Bank acted as lender of last resort to the banking system for the first time, by lending cash to banks that were temporarily unable to meet the demands of their depositors for withdrawals, during the financial crisis of 1866. The Bank declined to bail out Overend Gurney, whose collapse had precipitated the crisis. In 1890, however, the Bank organized a bailout of Baring Brothers and Company. The Bank of England was eventually nationalized (taken into public ownership) in 1946.

The first attempt to establish a government bank in the United States, the Bank of North America (1782), came almost a century after the creation of the Bank of England. It was succeeded by the First Bank of the United States (1791–1811) and the Second Bank of the United States (1816–36), both of which were refused renewals of their charters in the face of political opposition to the principle of federal (national) regulation of banking, as opposed to state regulation.

By contrast, the earliest US shareholder-owned commercial banks, the Bank of Massachusetts and the Bank of New York (both 1784), were formed and chartered at state level several decades before their English counterparts. The requirements for state chartering were eased during the 1830s leading to the 'free banking era' (1837–62), during which there was rapid growth in the banking industry, and an extension of a diverse patchwork of banknotes issued by state-chartered banks. Legislation passed in 1863 and 1864 allowed banks to be chartered at federal level, and created the conditions for the emergence of a unified national currency.

The 'national banking era' (1863–1913) saw the emergence of the dual system that operates in the US today, in which federally- and state-chartered banks coexist. Deprived of their powers to issue banknotes, the state-chartered banks survived by expanding deposit-taking, and benefitting from capital requirements that were generally lighter than those of federally-chartered banks. For much of the national banking area, federally-chartered banks and state-chartered banks in most states were subject to double, multiple, or unlimited shareholder liability. Under double liability, shareholders of failed banks could lose both their original investment, and an additional sum that usually approximated to the original investment. Under multiple or unlimited liability, shareholder exposure in the event of failure was even greater. Such provisions were intended to act as a brake on risky banking practice, but the national banking era still witnessed a series of banking and financial crises. One of the most severe, the Panic of 1907, provided the impetus for the creation of a federally-chartered central bank that could act as lender of last resort during a banking crisis. Legislation passed in 1913 established the modern-day Federal Reserve System (see Chapter 4).

During the early 1930s, as the Great Depression gathered momentum, the banking industry entered a phase of renewed crisis. Reform was a key component of the incoming Roosevelt administration's 'New Deal'. Following the temporary closure of all US banks for several days in March 1933, measures to restore confidence included the creation of the Federal Deposit Insurance Corporation (FDIC) to provide deposit insurance, a scheme guaranteeing that small depositors are reimbursed if their bank collapses; the extension of federal regulatory oversight to all banks for the first time; and the separation of commercial from investment banking under the provisions of the Glass–Steagall Act (1933). Double and multiple shareholder liability fell out of favour during the 1930s, and was replaced almost everywhere by limited liability.

The reforms of the 1930s, together with stable currency values maintained by the post-Second World War Bretton Woods system of fixed currency exchange rates, provided the foundation for a phase of relatively stable and tightly regulated banking during the 1940s, 1950s, and 1960s. The demise of Bretton Woods in 1973, and a growing trend towards the liberalization and deregulation of financial markets from the 1970s onwards, created opportunities for the development of new financial services, as well as new sources of risk that were brought sharply into focus by the global financial crisis of 2007–9.

In the US mutuals include Savings and Loan (S&L) associations, also known as thrifts. S&Ls first appeared during the 1830s, and were modelled on UK building societies. Members subscribed to shares, purchased in monthly instalments, and could borrow funds for a house purchase in proportion to their shareholdings. Interest was charged, and the loan was repaid through continued monthly payments. Urban growth during the second half of the 19th century was accompanied by a proliferation of S&Ls. Many S&Ls disappeared during the S&L crisis of the late 1980s and early 1990s, due primarily to unsound mortgage lending (see Chapter 6). Other mutuals in the US include savings banks, the first of which was formed in Boston in 1816; and credit unions, which originated in the early 20th century. Credit union membership, defined by a 'common bond', is restricted to individuals who share some form of association, such as an employer, profession, or church.

Structure of a bank's balance sheet and income statement

To understand what banks do and how they operate, it is useful to examine the structure of a typical bank's balance sheet and income statement. By law, all banks are required to publish these financial statements at regular intervals, usually either annually or quarterly. A balance sheet is a report on the financial structure and condition of a company, providing a realistic assessment of the value of the company's assets and liabilities at the time of publication.

Banks typically raise funds from depositors, investors, and their own shareholders. These funds are classed as liabilities on the bank's balance sheet, because they impose an obligation on the bank to service the funds it has effectively borrowed, for example by paying interest. They also impose an obligation on the bank to repay these funds at some point in the future, for example when a bond issued by the bank matures, or whenever a depositor chooses to withdraw funds or close an account.

When a depositor places funds in a personal or company bank account, the bank effectively borrows those funds from the depositor. In exchange, the bank incurs an obligation to provide various types of banking service and, in the case of savings accounts, pay interest on the funds deposited. A bond issued by a bank is a commitment on the part of the bank to make regular payments to the investor over the lifetime of the bond, equivalent to interest payments on the nominal value of the bond, and to repay the nominal value at a specified date of maturity. Typically the total amount repaid exceeds the initial purchase price of the bond, in order to provide the investor with a return. The issue of a bond is analogous to the bank borrowing funds from the bond purchaser or investor. The value of bonds the bank has issued but not yet redeemed appears as debt on the bank's balance sheet. The legal entitlement of bondholders to repayment in the event of the bank's failure is weaker than that of other creditors, including depositors, to whom the bank owes money. A hierarchy may also exist among the holders of different classes of bond. The holders of a class of bond known as 'subordinated debt' have the weakest protection, ranking below depositors and other bondholders in the queue for repayment if the bank is liquidated.

Banks apply or invest the funds they have raised from depositors, investors, and shareholders in several ways to build a portfolio of assets that generate profits for shareholders. Some of the funds raised by the bank may be held in liquid forms such as cash, or deposits with the central bank that can be converted back into cash rapidly if the need arises. Holdings of cash, and deposits that are highly liquid and secure, are known as reserves. The bank may also act as an investor, by purchasing bonds or other securities issued by private-sector companies or the government. A government bond is a security issued and sold by the government as a means to raise finance. In return for purchasing the bond, the investor receives a regular stream of interest or 'coupon' payments from the government, followed by redemption of the nominal value of the bond on the date of maturity. Unlike bonds sold by other issuers, such as private-sector companies, government bonds are usually believed to carry little or no risk of default, because the government, via the central bank, can always create the money it needs (see Chapter 4) in order to meet its commitments to its own bondholders.

Finally, some of the funds raised by the bank, often the largest proportion, may be used to grant loans to individuals or businesses, generating a future stream of interest payments from borrowers to the bank.

The difference between a bank's total assets, and its liabilities in the form of funds raised from depositors and investors, is the bank's capital, also known as equity or net worth. For a bank to remain solvent, the value of its assets must always exceed the value of its liabilities. Capital acts as a buffer against unanticipated losses. Capital or equity, which constitutes the shareholders' ownership stake in the bank, is also a source of funding for the bank, and therefore appears on the liabilities side of the balance sheet. Capital may derive from the original shareholders' financial investment in setting up the bank, or from past profits that have been retained, rather than paid out to shareholders as dividends.

Like any company, the stock market's valuation of a bank's capital or equity, given by the share price multiplied by the number of shares outstanding, might be above or below the value reported on the balance sheet, depending upon whether stock market investors and traders believe the balance sheet overstates or understates the bank's true worth.

Table 1 shows a summary aggregation of the balance sheets reported by all UK monetary financial institutions (MFIs), except the Bank of England, in December 2015. MFIs are institutions licensed to accept deposits, including branches of banks domiciled elsewhere in the European Economic Area, but not including credit unions, friendly societies, and insurance companies.

Banks earn profits by charging borrowers higher rates of interest than they pay depositors and other suppliers of funds, and by charging fees for a range of other financial services. A company's income statement reports the main components of income generated and costs incurred by the company over a specific period, and the profit (or loss) accruing to the company's shareholders. Table 2 shows a summary aggregate income statement for all UK MFIs in 2014. Numbers shown in parentheses in Table 2, and in other figures and tables throughout this book, represent negative values. Profitability measures include return on assets (ROA), defined as profit (or loss) expressed as a percentage of total assets; and return on equity (ROE), defined as profit (or loss) expressed as a percentage of capital or equity. Another profitability measure sometimes quoted is the net interest margin (NIM), defined as the difference between the average interest rate charged by the bank on its loans to borrowers, and the average interest rate paid by the bank to its depositors and other lenders.

Banking services

So far, banks have been characterized as financial intermediaries that specialize in accepting deposits from savers and granting loans to borrowers. Banks also provide a range of other financial services to their customers.

Retail banking covers the provision of banking services to individual consumers, households, and small firms, either on the high street or via phone or online. Banks that provide retail banking services accept deposits from households that are paid into current accounts or savings accounts. Current accounts, also sometimes known as cheque accounts, demand deposits or sight deposits, typically pay little or no interest, but allow the depositor to demand immediate withdrawal of funds. The bank incurs high costs in processing large volumes of small transactions, and in providing infrastructure such as high-street branches and automated teller machines (ATMs). In many countries banks impose a range of charges for routine current account transactions such as payment by cheque, or withdrawals from ATMs. In some countries there are no current account charges, provided the account remains in credit. Savings accounts, also known as time deposits, pay interest but may require a specified notice period before funds can be withdrawn.

On the lending side, lending to households may be either secured or unsecured. Mortgages are the principal category of secured loans to households, used to finance the purchase of property. The property acts as collateral, meaning that the bank has the right to take possession, should the borrower fail to make the scheduled payments and thereby default on the loan. Interest payments on mortgages may be either fixed for a certain period after the loan is taken out and variable thereafter, or variable throughout the entire term. A householder whose property exceeds in value the amount of any outstanding mortgage may opt to extract equity, by taking out a new mortgage secured against the excess value of the property, and using the proceeds to finance additional consumer spending or pay down other debt. Unsecured loans are used to finance the purchase of items such as cars or home improvements.

Table 1 UK monetary financial institutions, aggregate balance sheet in £bn (summary), December 2015

Assets			Liabilities		
Cash and balances at central banks		318	Deposits:		
			UK MFIs	474	
Loans and advances:			Other UK residents	2,195	
UK MFIs	466		Non-residents	1,998	4,667
Other UK residents	2,069				
Non-residents	1,898	4,433	Sale and repurchase agreements (repos):		
			UK MFIs	133	
Sale and repurchase agreements (repos):			Other UK residents	181	
UK MFIs	110		Non-residents	519	833
Other UK residents	229				
Non-residents	566	905	Certificates of deposit and commercial paper		195

Assets			Liabilities		
Bills including treasury bills		54	Bonds:		
Investments:			Maturity > 5 years	198	
UK government bonds	137		Maturity ≤ 5 years	254	452
UK MFIs	67		Other liabilities		118
Other UK residents	223				
Non-residents	521	948	Total liabilities		6,265
Other assets		205	Capital/equity		598
Total assets		**6,863**	**Total liabilities and capital**		**6,863**

Source: Bankstats (Monetary and Financial Statistics), Bank of England

Table 2 UK monetary financial institutions, aggregate income statement in £m (summary), 2014

Net interest income	59,167	
Dividends received	12,924	
Net fee and commission income	20,140	
Trading income	5,129	
Other income	26,205	
Total income		**123,565**
Staff costs	(32,507)	
Other operating expenses	(56,472)	
Total operating expenses		**(88,979)**
Profit before provisions		**34,586**
Net new provision charges	(1,085)	
Other items	(9,326)	
Profit before tax		**24,175**
Tax	(5,403)	
Dividends paid	(6,151)	
Other items	(513)	
Retained profit		**12,108**

Source: Bankstats (Monetary and Financial Statistics), Bank of England

There is no collateral for the bank to seize if the borrower defaults. Interest may be either fixed or variable.

Lending to small businesses typically takes the form of overdrafts or term loans. An overdraft is an arrangement allowing the business to withdraw funds exceeding the current balance on the account up to a specified limit. The bank charges interest on the amount overdrawn, and may also charge an arrangement fee.

A term loan is a business loan with a specified maturity (at least one year, and typically several years) and a schedule of interest and capital repayments.

Retail banking also covers the provision of several other financial services. These include: safe-keeping services, the provision of secure means for storing wealth; and accounting services, the creation and maintenance of records of each customer's financial transactions. Other retail banking services include stockbroking, insurance, foreign exchange transactions, pensions, leasing, and hire purchase.

Wholesale banking covers the provision of financial services to large firms or corporations, including both non-financial and financial firms (other banks, and non-bank financial institutions). Wholesale banking subdivides into corporate banking and investment banking.

Corporate banking covers the provision of core banking services to large firms or corporations. Core banking services include accepting deposits and granting loans, as well as a range of specialized banking services for corporations. There are a number of methods banks can use to lend to large firms or corporations. A bank may extend a line of credit, allowing the corporation to borrow and repay flexibly, subject to a maximum amount that may be borrowed within any given period. A revolving credit facility provides similar borrowing flexibility, but usually on a larger scale. When a corporation wishes to borrow a larger sum than its bank is willing or able to lend, the bank may organize a syndicated loan, by making arrangements for several other banks or other lenders to contribute to the loan jointly. Syndicated lending is typically long term. Finally, banks may provide long-term finance for large investment projects undertaken by corporations, by lending or purchasing bonds issued by special purpose vehicles (SPVs) set up by the corporation running the project. The corporation holds an ownership (equity) stake in the SPV. In addition to corporate lending, banks also provide other specialized financial services for their corporate clients. These include issuing guarantees, interest rate and foreign exchange rate risk management, and financing overseas trade.

Investment banking covers the provision of specialized banking and financial services, primarily to corporate customers, but also to wealthy private individuals and to governments. Investment banking also includes a number of trading activities on financial markets. Advisory services include the provision of advice and assistance in arranging mergers and acquisitions, and various other consultancy services. Investment banking also covers the provision of assistance to privately owned companies with stock market flotation, or governments with the privatization of state-owned companies. Underwriting of new issues of securities (corporate bonds, equities, or government bonds) usually involves a syndicate of investment banks each taking responsibility for selling an allocation of the new issue, and retaining its allocation if it fails to find a buyer. Investment banks are also involved in the provision of asset and wealth management services, and trading in securities, commodities, and derivatives (see Chapter 3), either on the bank's own behalf (known as proprietary trading) or on behalf of corporate or private customers.

Types of bank

A commercial bank is defined as one whose main business is financial intermediation: accepting deposits and granting loans. Customers of commercial banks include individuals, small businesses, and larger firms or corporations. Accordingly, commercial banks supply both retail banking and corporate banking services. Most commercial banks are owned by shareholders, and seek to earn a profit in order to provide shareholders with a return on their investment in the bank's capital (equity).

An investment bank specializes in providing investment banking services. Typically, an investment bank comprises an advisory division, specializing in underwriting, stock market flotations, and other consultancy services; and a trading division, specializing in trading on financial markets, and asset management. Most investment banks are also shareholder-owned and therefore profit-motivated.

In practice, the distinction between commercial banks and investment banks is not as clear as these definitions might suggest. In the US, the Glass–Steagall Act (1933) separated commercial banking from investment banking, by preventing affiliations between commercial and investment banks that would have allowed the latter to trade in funds raised from deposits taken by the former. This legal separation was eventually terminated by the Gramm–Leach–Bliley Act (1999). Subsequently, commercial banks have become involved in securities trading, and some investment banks have accepted deposits and granted loans. Several mergers between US commercial banks and investment banks have led to the creation of universal banks, providing the full range of commercial and investment banking services.

In many countries, retail banking services are supplied not only by commercial banks, but also by a range of mutually-owned, rather than shareholder-owned, institutions. The nature of the mutuals varies between the countries in which they operate: prominent examples include the few surviving UK building societies that avoided demutualization through acquisition or conversion to shareholder-owned banks; and the US S&Ls (thrifts). A defining characteristic of mutuals is that each institution is owned by its own members, who are also the depositors and borrowers. Mutuals earn surpluses, rather than profits, which are either distributed to the members or retained to finance expansion. In principle, since there is no shareholder profit, mutuals should be able to offer more competitive interest rates to depositors and borrowers than shareholder-owned commercial banks.

In 2016 the four largest US banks by total assets (the value of all outstanding loans, together with other investments including shares, bonds, property, and cash shown on their balance sheets) were JPMorgan Chase ($2,424bn total assets in 2016), Bank of America ($2,186bn), Wells Fargo ($1,849bn), and Citigroup ($1,801bn). These can all be described as universal banks. The next two, Goldman Sachs ($878bn) and Morgan Stanley ($807bn), are investment banks that hurriedly converted to deposit-taking status at the height of the financial crisis in 2008, in order to qualify for public bailout funds (see Chapter 7).

The UK banking industry is dominated by five large independent banks, HSBC ($2,596bn total assets in 2016), Barclays ($1,795bn), Royal Bank of Scotland (RBS) ($1,269bn), Lloyds ($1,185bn), and Standard Chartered ($640bn). The first four from this list, together with the wholly-owned UK subsidiary of the Spanish banking group Banco Santander, dominate UK retail banking. The fifth independent bank, Standard Chartered, operates mainly overseas in Asia and the Middle East, Africa, and Latin America.

The universal banking model characterizes the largest shareholder-owned banks in several other European countries where, historically, there was no regulatory divide between commercial and investment banking. In 2016 the six largest Eurozone banks were BNP Paribas (France, $2,404bn total assets in 2016), Deutsche Bank (Germany, $1,973bn), Crédit Agricole (France, $1,858bn), Société Générale (France, $1,550bn), Banco Santander (Spain, $1,501bn), and Groupe BPCE (France, $1,357bn).

In 2016 HSBC, JPMorgan Chase, BNP Paribas, Bank of America, and Deutsche Bank were ranked sixth to tenth, respectively, in the list of the world's largest banks by asset size. Four of the top five banks were Chinese: Industrial and Commercial Bank of China (ICBC) ($3,545bn total assets in 2016), China Construction Bank ($2,966bn), Agricultural Bank of China ($2,853bn), and Bank of

China ($2,640bn). The list of the world's five largest banks is completed by the Japanese bank Mitsubishi UFJ Financial Group ($2,655bn).

The shadow banking system

In addition to financial services providers that are licensed and regulated as banks, many other companies or other institutions are involved in financial intermediation activities, which take place outside the traditional banking system. In some cases, banks themselves have set up subsidiaries, known as Special Purpose Vehicles (SPVs) or Structured Investment Vehicles (SIVs), to transact business that would be regulated more intrusively if the activity was channelled through the parent bank, rather than the subsidiary. The term 'shadow banking' was coined by Paul McCulley of the asset management company PIMCO in 2007 to describe 'the whole alphabet soup of levered up non-bank investment conduits, vehicles, and structures'. The shadow banking sector includes the following types of institution.

A hedge fund pools the funds of its investors to purchase securities. Hedge funds may be structured as partnerships or limited liability companies. A hedge fund is administered by a professional management team, which may adopt a specific investment style or specialize in particular securities. Investors are charged a management fee. Unlike mutual funds, hedge funds can borrow and use leverage (see Chapter 2) to achieve a preferred combination of expected return and risk for investors.

An exchange-traded fund (ETF) purchases assets such as shares, bonds, or commodities on behalf of its investors. Most ETFs track a particular market index, guaranteeing to match the index's performance, and are traded in the relevant market. Since the investment strategy is passive, management fees are minimal.

A Special Purpose Vehicle (SPV) is a subsidiary of a financial institution, with its own legal status that protects it from insolvency in the event that the parent institution becomes insolvent. An SPV is usually set up to deal in specific assets or liabilities, and may be used by the parent to remove these items from its own balance sheet, perhaps evading the need to hold capital as a buffer to absorb possible losses on the assets concerned. Such items are said to be held off-balance sheet. A Structured Investment Vehicle (SIV) is a type of SPV, which deals in structured securities (see Chapter 3).

A private equity company hires investment professionals to make investments in the equity of other companies, with the aim of delivering a high return to the company's own shareholders.

An asset management company offers services in managing the investments, including bonds, shares, and property, of wealthy individuals. A wealth management company performs similar functions, but with stronger emphasis on investment and tax advisory services and financial planning.

A money market fund (MMF) is a mutual fund that invests in short-term securities such as Treasury Bills (short-term government bonds) and commercial paper (short-term bonds or promissory notes issued by large corporations). A money market fund aims to provide investors with a higher yield than a bank deposit, but at very low risk. In the US an MMF seeks to maintain a stable net asset value (NAV) of $1 per share, by returning any earnings beyond what is required to maintain a stable NAV to investors, in the form of dividends.

In the US a broker-dealer is a brokerage that trades in securities on behalf of clients and on its own account. Broker-dealers range in size from small independents to large subsidiaries of commercial or investment banks.

In the US a real-estate investment trust (REIT) is a company that owns and manages commercial property such as offices, warehouses, shopping malls, hotels, apartment blocks, or hospitals. REITs provide investors with opportunities to invest in property, on a similar basis to mutual funds.

Shadow banking institutions are not licensed as banks, and are not subject to the same supervisory and regulatory arrangements. However, licensed banks and shadow banking institutions are closely connected in many ways, apart from ownership relationships in the case of SPVs. For example, banks and shadow banking institutions both trade in markets for short-term funding (see Chapter 3). The failure of a large shadow banking institution could have serious consequences for the stability of interconnected banks. This explains the nervousness of the regulatory authorities about the growth of shadow banking in recent decades. In the US shadow banking assets are estimated to exceed those of traditional banks. Globally the shadow banking system (defined as non-bank financial intermediation) held assets of around $75 trillion in 2013, or approximately half of the assets of all banks.

The payments system

The payments system is the banking infrastructure for the processing and settlement of financial transactions between people and organizations. For many decades, the cheque ('check' in the US) was the most important component of the payments system. A cheque is an instruction from a customer to his bank to transfer funds from the customer's account to the account of the payee named on the cheque. Cheques allow transactions to take place without transferring large amounts of currency. If the two accounts are held with the same bank, the bank settles the transaction itself. If the two accounts are held with different banks, the transaction is processed through a central clearing system. Standing orders and direct debits are used to facilitate recurring payments. With a standing order the customer instructs the bank to pay a specified amount into another account on specified dates. With a direct debit, the payee can vary the amounts and dates of the recurring payments.

In the UK the clearing banks, full members of the Cheque and Credit Clearing Company, are responsible for processing cheques drawn on or credited to their customers' accounts. In addition to the Bank of England, the UK clearing banks are Bank of Scotland, Barclays, Clydesdale, Cooperative, HSBC, Lloyds, NatWest, Nationwide Building Society, Royal Bank of Scotland (RBS), and Santander UK. Non-clearing banks typically enter into commercially negotiated agency agreements with one of the clearing banks in order to provide chequing services to their account holders. In the UK Bacs Payment Schemes Limited (formerly Bankers Automated Clearing Systems) operates the clearing and settlement of automated payments, such as direct debit, direct from one bank account to another.

With the growth of computer technology and the expansion of the internet, the payments system has been extended to include ATMs (automated teller machines), debit and credit cards, electronic transfer of funds, and electronic payments systems such as PayPal and Bitcoin. ATMs allow bank customers to withdraw cash from their accounts without visiting a bank branch. The first ATM was introduced by Barclays in London in 1967. Debit cards, normally enabled for use with ATMs, also allow retailers to accept payments direct from the customer's bank account. In the UK the retailer processes the transaction through an EFTPOS (electronic funds transfer at the point of sale) terminal. Credit cards allow customers to pay for goods and services using funds that are effectively loaned by the credit card company. The customer receives a monthly statement, and may choose to pay off the full balance, or pay a portion and incur interest on the balance. Smart cards allow customers to load funds onto a plastic card, which can be debited directly by a retailer. Telephone banking and internet banking provide facilities for customers to transact with their banks without visiting a bank branch. Average costs per transaction for the bank are typically a small proportion of the cost of transactions through branches. Recently, mobile payments technologies have been introduced to allow customers to pay for goods and services through their smartphones or tablets.

Chapter 2
Financial intermediation

The term financial intermediation refers to the traditional banking business model, under which a bank accepts deposits from savers and lends funds to borrowers. The accumulation of bank deposits and the growth of bank lending are inextricably linked. Whenever a bank grants a loan, it credits the borrower's account with a deposit equivalent to the amount lent and borrowed. The borrower then spends the funds, which reappear elsewhere in the banking system as a deposit made by the provider of the goods or services the loan was used to pay for. Likewise, whenever a bank receives a deposit, it has the option of using the funds to support additional lending to those of its customers who are seeking to borrow.

Maturity transformation, size transformation, and diversification

In its role as financial intermediary, the bank performs the functions of maturity transformation, size transformation, and diversification. Maturity transformation refers to the preference of savers to be able to withdraw their money at any time, while borrowers retain the right not to repay until the loan matures. Liquidity refers to the ease or speed at which an asset can be converted to cash. Bank deposits are liquid: making a deposit entails only a short-term commitment on the part of the depositor.

By contrast, when a bank grants a loan, for example a mortgage to finance a house purchase, or a business loan to finance investment in new capital equipment, the bank's commitment is long-term and illiquid.

Size transformation refers to the bank's task of simultaneously managing a large portfolio of bank deposits that are small in average value, and a smaller portfolio of loans that are typically much larger in average value. Diversification refers to the benefits depositors gain by pooling risk, when their funds support loans granted to a range of borrowers. From past experience the bank knows that a certain proportion of its loans will default and never be repaid. The interest rates charged to borrowers include a margin sufficient to cover the average losses incurred by the bank through defaults. In this way, provided the actual rate of default turns out to be in line with the bank's expectations, the depositors' funds are secure. Each depositor would not achieve the same security if he lent directly to an individual borrower, because the risk would be concentrated entirely on one party, rather than spread over many borrowers.

Although financial intermediation services are widely seen as crucial for an efficiently functioning financial system, in recent years the traditional banking business model has been challenged by the growth of alternative models for saving and borrowing, such as peer-to-peer lending (P2PL). A for-profit intermediary company offering P2PL sets up an online platform, which brings together individual lenders and borrowers. Lenders may compete to offer each borrower the cheapest rate, or the intermediary may set the rate based on an assessment of the borrower's creditworthiness. Most loans are unsecured, and lenders typically offset risk by diversifying (lending to different borrowers). The intermediary earns a profit by charging fees to lenders and borrowers. Volumes of P2PL business are small relative to traditional financial intermediation, and the scale of the threat to traditional banking remains an open question.

Adverse selection, moral hazard, and financial transactions

Traders in any market need information for the market to work effectively. For example, both buyers and sellers need to know about the characteristics of the product or service being traded, in order to strike a fair price. Asymmetric information, when one party to a transaction has more information than the other party, hinders the smooth functioning of markets. Markets for financial intermediation services are particularly susceptible to problems of asymmetric information, in the form of adverse selection and moral hazard.

Adverse selection occurs when a service is chosen predominantly by a group of buyers who offer a poor return to the company selling the service. In financial intermediation the problem arises because the borrowers have better information about themselves than the lender, and the lender encounters difficulties in distinguishing between reliable borrowers and unreliable ones. For example, suppose a bank is considering one-year loan applications from a pool of borrowers, half of whom are reliable, carrying only a 2 per cent risk of default (failing to repay the loan) at the end of one year, while the other half are unreliable, carrying a 10 per cent default risk. The bank would like to set the interest rates on the loans in a way that protects itself from potential losses arising from default. If the bank can accurately distinguish between reliable and unreliable borrowers, it can do so easily, by charging the former an interest rate that includes a 2 per cent margin to cover the risk of default, and the latter a 10 per cent margin. If the bank is unable to distinguish, however, it faces a dilemma in deciding what margin to charge:

If the bank charges a 2 per cent margin, it will be under-protected because some of the borrowers actually carry a 10 per cent default risk.

If the bank charges a 6 per cent margin, equivalent to the average default risk, unreliable borrowers feel they are getting a good deal, but reliable borrowers feel they are being overcharged and will look elsewhere for a cheaper loan. The bank fails to strike any contracts with reliable borrowers; and worse, is left with the unreliable borrowers on its books, paying a margin of 6 per cent but carrying a default risk of 10 per cent. The bank can expect to record losses over a large number of similar contracts.

If the bank charges a 10 per cent margin, reliable borrowers look elsewhere as before, but unreliable borrowers remain and pay a fair price. The bank fails to transact with any borrower carrying a lower default risk than the least reliable (hence the term 'adverse' selection).

If all banks face similar difficulties, the reliable borrowers may be unable to find any bank willing to lend at a rate they would accept. In other words, reliable borrowers may be unable to obtain credit, a situation known as credit rationing. For banks, the solution lies in collecting the information needed to distinguish between reliable and unreliable borrowers. A bank might screen its loan applicants to reveal the information it requires. Two models for screening have been proposed; in practice a bank may use a combination of both. With transactional banking the bank relies on standardized information for a large number of borrowers, in the form of responses to questions on a loan application form, or personal credit scores obtained by the bank from a credit-rating company. With relationship banking the bank gathers information on its customers individually, by developing a long-term relationship for the provision of financial services. The bank gets to know its customers by observing patterns of cash flows through their accounts, or by meeting them individually to discuss aspects of financial planning.

The second type of asymmetric information problem, moral hazard, refers to a tendency for one person to behave irresponsibly, in the knowledge that someone else will bear the cost of their risky or negligent behaviour. The opportunity to behave irresponsibly may arise when one party to a financial transaction has more information about his own intentions or actions than the other. For example, after the contract between lender and borrower for a bank loan has been agreed, the borrower might have insufficient incentive to manage his financial affairs prudently if it is the lender, not the borrower, who ultimately bears the cost if the borrower encounters financial difficulties and defaults on the loan.

To address a moral hazard problem, the bank could attempt to monitor the customer's actions. However, it may be difficult for the bank to observe closely how the customer is using the borrowed funds. In the case of secured lending, the borrower is required to pledge collateral, which the borrower forfeits if the loan defaults. Alternatively, the lender could include restrictive covenants in the contract with the borrower: for example, specifying that the loan can only be used for a particular purpose; or requiring a corporate borrower to keep a certain proportion of its assets in a form that can be sold easily.

Most financial transactions are susceptible to problems of asymmetric information in the form of adverse selection and moral hazard. In the case of bank lending, asymmetric information is a key source of credit risk, the risk that the borrower will fail to meet his obligations to make repayments, causing the bank to incur losses.

Leverage, and the magnification of return and risk

Leverage, defined as the amount of debt a company uses to finance its assets, is another fundamental cause of the fragility of banks. A bank adds leverage whenever it borrows in order to finance risky investments, including the granting of loans to borrowers (a form of investment from the bank's perspective). Leverage magnifies shareholder profits if things go according to plan, but leverage can also jeopardize a bank's solvency if things go wrong.

The following example illustrates how leverage works in the case of an individual borrowing from a bank by taking out a mortgage. Suppose an individual has accumulated savings of £100,000, which he intends to use towards the purchase of a house. Option 1 is for the householder to borrow £100,000 from the bank and purchase a house costing £200,000. If the value of the house subsequently increases by 10 per cent to £220,000, the householder's equity increases by 20 per cent from £100,000 to £120,000; if the value of the house drops by 10 per cent to £180,000, the equity shrinks by 20 per cent from £100,000 to £80,000. If the house value were to drop by 20 per cent, the equity would shrink by 40 per cent to £60,000. Under Option 1 the householder has modest leverage, because the initial value of the loan is only 50 per cent of the value of the house. Even modest leverage, however, magnifies the effect of swings in the value of the underlying asset on the value of the householder's equity stake in the house.

Option 2 is for the householder to borrow £500,000 from the bank and purchase a house costing £600,000. If the value of the house subsequently increases by 10 per cent to £660,000, the householder's equity increases by 60 per cent from £100,000 to £160,000; if the value of the house drops by 10 per cent to £540,000, the equity shrinks by 60 per cent from £100,000 to £40,000. Under Option 2 the householder has higher leverage, because the initial value of the loan is 83 per cent of the value of the house. Accordingly the magnification effect is much larger. If the value of the house were to drop by 20 per cent, the equity would be wiped out, because the house value of £480,000 would be less than the loan of £500,000.

The example shows how leverage magnifies risk for an individual taking out a mortgage. However, banks themselves increase leverage whenever they raise funds from depositors or investors, in order to grant loans that may amount in value to a large multiple of shareholder capital or equity. Leverage multiplies the rate of profit earned by shareholders when the bank's loans and investments outperform expectations. However, leverage also increases risk. If the bank's loans or investments underperform, leverage magnifies losses, possibly jeopardizing the bank's solvency.

Credit risk and liquidity risk

By acting as a financial intermediary, a bank takes on several types of risk. The two most fundamental types of risk are credit risk and liquidity risk. Credit risk refers to the risk that a borrower will fail to meet his obligations to make repayments to the bank. When a loan becomes delinquent, meaning there is no prospect of the borrower being able to repay, the bank must reduce the value of the assets shown on its balance sheet. An equivalent reduction must also be shown on the liabilities side of the balance sheet, by reducing the bank's capital. Capital therefore provides a buffer or cushion, enabling the bank to absorb losses on its loans or other investments. If the bank's capital is wiped out altogether by losses on loans or other investments, the bank becomes insolvent.

A useful measure of a bank's loss-absorbing capacity is the capital-to-assets ratio, sometimes known as the capital ratio, defined as the ratio of the bank's capital to its total assets. Leverage, sometimes known alternatively as gearing, is measured by the reciprocal of the capital ratio: total assets divided by capital. A bank with a capital ratio of 10 per cent operates with a leverage of 10 (the bank's total assets are ten times its capital), and could absorb a 10 per cent drop in the value of its assets and still have sufficient assets to cover its liabilities. A bank with a capital ratio of 5 per cent operates with a leverage of 20, and could only absorb a 5 per cent drop in the value of its assets and remain solvent. The higher the leverage, the smaller is the capital buffer and the greater is the risk of insolvency.

The bank's management often faces a conflict between the competing objectives of maximizing the bank's profitability, and minimizing the risk of insolvency. The following example compares the financial structure and performance of two banks, known as Lo-Risk Bank and Hi-Risk Bank. The assumptions are as follows:

First, both banks charge interest at 4 per cent per year on their loans. This rate is fixed for one year.

Second, both banks currently pay their depositors interest at a rate of 1.5 per cent per year. This rate may vary if market interest rates change. Market rates are expected to remain unchanged.

Third, both banks earn a return of 2 per cent per year on their investments in securities.

Fourth, both banks expect their investments in securities to remain unchanged in value from year to year.

Fifth, both banks pay interest of 2 per cent per year on their debt.

Sixth, and finally, both banks include under their costs an allowance for expected losses from borrower defaults equivalent to 2 per cent of the value of their loans portfolios. During the course of each year, both banks grant new loans equivalent in value to their expected defaults, and both banks therefore expect the total value of their loans portfolios to remain constant from year to year.

For simplicity the value of the banks' physical assets are not included on their balance sheets, and their operating costs are not included on their income statements. Lo-Risk Bank operates with assets of 100, and capital of 8, resulting in a capital ratio of 8 per cent and leverage of 12.5. Hi-Risk Bank operates with assets of 200, capital of 8, a capital ratio of 4 per cent, and leverage of 25.

Figure 2 shows the opening balance sheets, income statements, and closing balance sheets of both banks for one year, during which the outcomes for both banks are precisely in accordance with their expectations. Lo-Risk Bank achieves a profit of 0.4, and a return on assets (ROA) of 0.4 per cent on assets of 100. Hi-Risk Bank achieves a profit of 0.6, and an ROA of 0.3 per cent on assets of 200. Lo-Risk Bank has a return on equity (ROE) of 5 per cent (profit of 0.4 on capital of 8), while Hi-Risk Bank has an ROE of 7.5 per cent (profit of 0.6 on capital of 8). Lo-Risk Bank's capital base of 8 supports total assets of 100, while Hi-Risk Bank maintains the same capital base to support assets of 200. Lo-Risk Bank achieves the higher ROA, but Hi-Risk Bank achieves the higher ROE. ROE is more important for shareholders than ROA. Shareholders are interested in the return on their ownership (equity) stake; and in this respect, the shareholders of Hi-Risk Bank are better rewarded than those of Lo-Risk Bank. The example shows that leverage is beneficial for shareholders when performance is in accordance with expectations. When things go wrong, however, a bank with more leverage is at greater risk of insolvency. Rather than focus solely on ROE, sophisticated investors may consider a risk-adjusted rate of return, taking into account the risks associated with the bank's balance sheet structure and investment strategy.

The implications of credit risk can be explored by running a stress test, summarized in Figure 3. Suppose the actual losses from loan defaults are 10 per cent of the value of the opening loans portfolios of both banks, rather than 2 per cent as the banks originally expected. Lo-Risk Bank, which has budgeted for loan-losses of 1.4 and will grant new loans corresponding to this amount, incurs a loan-loss outcome of 7. This wipes out Lo-Risk Bank's profit of 0.4, creating a loss of 5.2. The drop in the value of Lo-Risk Bank's loans portfolio from 70 to 64.4 (= opening value of 70, *minus* defaults of 7, *plus* new loans of 1.4) is matched on the closing balance sheet by the depletion of Lo-Risk Bank's capital, from 8 to 2.4. Although its capital base is weakened, Lo-Risk Bank is able to withstand the losses, and remains solvent.

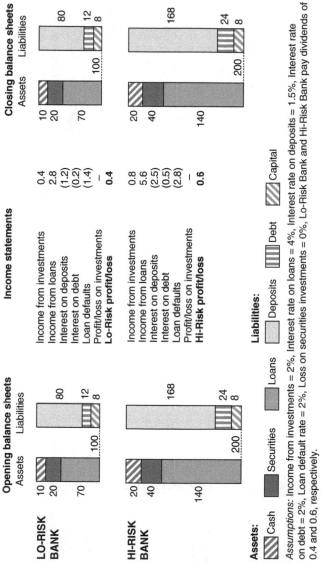

Opening balance sheets

LO-RISK BANK

Assets / Liabilities

Assets: Cash 10, Securities 20, Loans 70 — 100
Liabilities: Deposits 80, Debt 12, Capital 8

HI-RISK BANK

Assets: Cash 20, Securities 40, Loans 140 — 200
Liabilities: Deposits 168, Debt 24, Capital 8

Income statements

Income from investments	0.4
Income from loans	2.8
Interest on deposits	(1.2)
Interest on debt	(0.2)
Loan defaults	(1.4)
Profit/loss on investments	–
Lo-Risk profit/loss	**0.4**

Income from investments	0.8
Income from loans	5.6
Interest on deposits	(2.5)
Interest on debt	(0.5)
Loan defaults	(2.8)
Profit/loss on investments	–
Hi-Risk profit/loss	**0.6**

Closing balance sheets

Assets / Liabilities

LO-RISK BANK: Assets: Cash 10, Securities 20, Loans 70 — 100
Liabilities: Deposits 80, Debt 12, Capital 8

HI-RISK BANK: Assets: Cash 20, Securities 40, Loans 140 — 200
Liabilities: Deposits 168, Debt 24, Capital 8

Assets: Cash, Securities, Loans

Liabilities: Deposits, Debt, Capital

Assumptions: Income from investments = 2%, Interest rate on loans = 4%, Interest rate on deposits = 1.5%, Interest rate on debt = 2%, Loan default rate = 2%, Loss on securities investments = 0%, Lo-Risk Bank and Hi-Risk Bank pay dividends of 0.4 and 0.6, respectively.

2. Balance sheet structures: Lo-Risk Bank and Hi-Risk Bank.

35

Banking

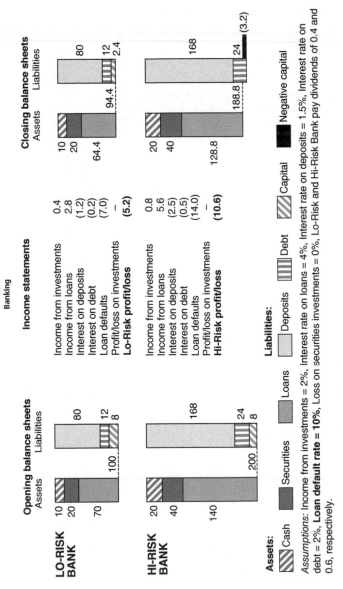

Opening balance sheets

LO-RISK BANK

Assets	Liabilities
Cash 10	80
Securities 20	12
Loans 70	8
Total 100

HI-RISK BANK

Assets	Liabilities
Cash 20	168
Securities 40	24
Loans 140	8
Total 200

Income statements

Income from investments	0.4
Income from loans	2.8
Interest on deposits	(1.2)
Interest on debt	(0.2)
Loan defaults	(7.0)
Profit/loss on investments	–
Lo-Risk profit/loss	**(5.2)**

Income from investments	0.8
Income from loans	5.6
Interest on deposits	(2.5)
Interest on debt	(0.5)
Loan defaults	(14.0)
Profit/loss on investments	–
Hi-Risk profit/loss	**(10.6)**

Closing balance sheets

Assets	Liabilities
10	80
20	12
64.4	2.4
94.4

Assets	Liabilities
20	168
40	24
128.8	(3.2)
188.8

Assets: Cash ▨ | Securities ▨ | Loans ▨

Liabilities: Deposits ▨ | Debt ▨ | Capital ▨ | Negative capital ▨

Assumptions: Income from investments = 2%, Interest rate on loans = 4%, Interest rate on deposits = 1.5%, Interest rate on debt = 2%, **Loan default rate = 10%**, Loss on securities investments = 0%, Lo-Risk and Hi-Risk Bank pay dividends of 0.4 and 0.6, respectively.

3. **Credit risk: Lo-Risk Bank and Hi-Risk Bank.**

For Hi-Risk Bank, the outcome is worse. Hi-Risk Bank, which has budgeted for loan losses of 2.8 and will create new loans corresponding to this amount, incurs a loan-loss outcome of 14. This wipes out Hi-Risk Bank's expected profit of 0.6, creating a loss of –10.6. The drop in the value of Hi-Risk Bank's loans portfolio from 140 to 128.8 (= original value of 140, *minus* defaults of 14, *plus* new loans of 2.8) is sufficient to wipe out Hi-Risk Bank's capital base of 8. Hi-Risk Bank is insolvent, with negative capital (an excess of liabilities over assets) of –3.2. Owing to its higher leverage, Hi-Risk Bank is wiped out by the unexpected losses on its loans portfolio.

Liquidity risk refers to the possibility that a bank might not hold sufficient assets in liquid form, either cash or deposits that can be converted to cash at very short notice, to be able to meet the demands of its depositors for immediate withdrawal of their funds. By itself, liquidity risk may not necessarily threaten the bank's underlying solvency, but a liquidity shortage may nevertheless have devastating consequences. If depositors lose confidence that they can access their funds on demand, panic may set in, and the demand for withdrawals may rapidly increase. It would be tempting to attempt to raise the funds needed to resolve a liquidity crisis by selling other assets, such as securities and loans. However, the enforced 'fire sale' of such assets at short notice might be possible only at heavily discounted prices, causing the liquidity crisis to mutate into a solvency crisis as the losses translate into depletion of the bank's capital. Once depositor confidence is undermined, it may be impossible for the bank's management to regain control without assistance from the central bank. Central bank assistance may involve issuing guarantees of deposits, or providing the funds needed to allow depositors to access their funds on demand.

A bank can reduce its liquidity risk exposure by holding more of its assets in liquid form, such as cash or deposits at the central bank. However, assets held in liquid form typically produce a smaller return than assets held in the form of loans or securities. Increasing the proportion of assets tied up in liquid form may reduce a bank's liquidity risk exposure, but it also reduces the bank's profitability.

Other sources of risk in financial intermediation

Credit risk and liquidity risk are not the only types of risk associated with financial intermediation. Market risk refers to the possibility that a bank's investments in securities might fail to deliver the returns expected, or the securities might fall in value. Figure 4 summarizes a stress test that examines the implications for Lo-Risk Bank and Hi-Risk Bank. Suppose the securities portfolios of both banks experience an unexpected drop in market value of 25 per cent, and are written down to their new market values on the closing balance sheets. In both cases, the drop in the value of assets is matched on the balance sheets by an equivalent depletion of capital. Lo-Risk Bank, which holds a securities portfolio initially valued at 20 and written down to 15, is able to withstand the loss of 5 by writing down its capital from 8 to 3, and remains solvent. Hi-Risk Bank, which holds a securities portfolio initially valued at 40 and written down to 30, is unable to withstand the loss of 10, and its opening capital base of 8 is wiped out. Owing to its higher leverage and as before, Hi-Risk Bank is rendered insolvent.

Interest-rate risk refers to the possibility that market interest rates might increase, obliging a bank to pay higher interest to their depositors, while the interest received from borrowers remains unchanged for loans with interest rates that the bank cannot alter immediately. Figure 5 summarizes a stress test. Suppose there is a sharp and unexpected increase in the market interest rate, requiring both banks to pay interest of 7.5 per cent on their deposits, rather than 1.5 per cent as anticipated. By contrast, the banks are locked in to charging interest of 4 per cent on their existing loans. This loss depletes the cash holdings of both banks. Lo-Risk Bank's unexpected additional interest expense is 4.8, and

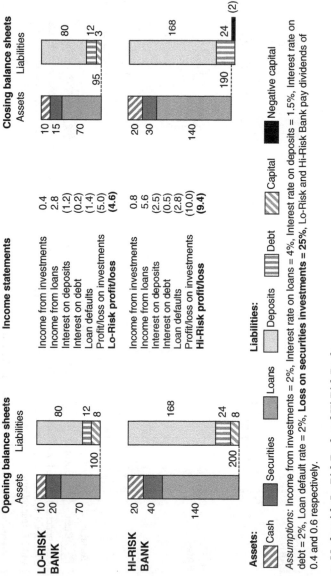

Opening balance sheets

LO-RISK BANK

Assets | Liabilities
Cash 10, Securities 20, Loans 70 = 100 | Deposits 80, Debt 12, Capital 8

HI-RISK BANK

Assets | Liabilities
Cash 20, Securities 40, Loans 140 = 200 | Deposits 168, Debt 24, Capital 8

Income statements

Income from investments	0.4
Income from loans	2.8
Interest on deposits	(1.2)
Interest on debt	(0.2)
Loan defaults	(1.4)
Profit/loss on investments	(5.0)
Lo-Risk profit/loss	**(4.6)**

Income from investments	0.8
Income from loans	5.6
Interest on deposits	(2.5)
Interest on debt	(0.5)
Loan defaults	(2.8)
Profit/loss on investments	(10.0)
Hi-Risk profit/loss	**(9.4)**

Closing balance sheets

Assets | Liabilities

LO-RISK Assets: Cash 10, 15, 70 = 95 | Liabilities: 80, 12, 3

HI-RISK Assets: 20, 30, 140 = 190 | Liabilities: 168, 24, (2)

Assets:

Cash — Securities — Loans

Liabilities:

Deposits — Debt — Capital — Negative capital

Assumptions: Income from investments = 2%, Interest rate on loans = 4%, Interest rate on deposits = 1.5%, Interest rate on debt = 2%, Loan default rate = 2%, **Loss on securities investments = 25%**, Lo-Risk and Hi-Risk Bank pay dividends of 0.4 and 0.6 respectively.

4. Market risk: Lo-Risk Bank and Hi-Risk Bank.

39

Banking

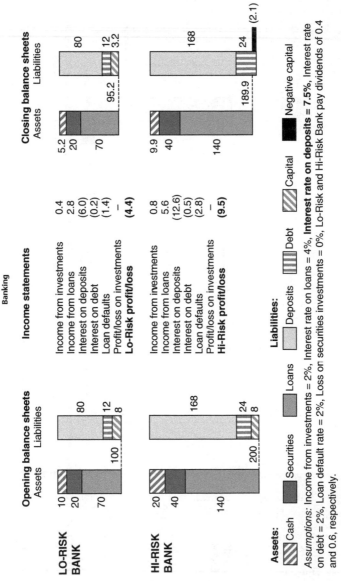

Opening balance sheets

Closing balance sheets

Income statements

LO-RISK BANK

Assets / Liabilities (Opening):
- Cash: 10
- Securities: 20
- Loans: 70 / 100
- Deposits: 80
- Debt: 12
- Capital: 8

Income statement (Lo-Risk):
Income from investments	0.4
Income from loans	2.8
Interest on deposits	(6.0)
Interest on debt	(0.2)
Loan defaults	(1.4)
Profit/loss on investments	–
Lo-Risk profit/loss	**(4.4)**

Assets / Liabilities (Closing):
- Cash: 5.2
- Securities: 20
- Loans: 70 / 95.2
- Deposits: 80
- Debt: 12
- Capital: 3.2

HI-RISK BANK

Assets / Liabilities (Opening):
- Cash: 20
- Securities: 40
- Loans: 140 / 200
- Deposits: 168
- Debt: 24
- Capital: 8

Income statement (Hi-Risk):
Income from investments	0.8
Income from loans	5.6
Interest on deposits	(12.6)
Interest on debt	(0.5)
Loan defaults	(2.8)
Profit/loss on investments	–
Hi-Risk profit/loss	**(9.5)**

Assets / Liabilities (Closing):
- Cash: 9.9
- Securities: 40
- Loans: 140 / 189.9
- Deposits: 168
- Debt: 24
- Capital: (2.1)

Assets:
Cash / Securities / Loans

Liabilities:
Deposits / Debt / Capital / Negative capital

Assumptions: Income from investments = 2%, Interest rate on loans = 4%, **Interest rate on deposits = 7.5%**, Interest rate on debt = 2%, Loan default rate = 2%, Loss on securities investments = 0%, Lo-Risk and Hi-Risk Bank pay dividends of 0.4 and 0.6, respectively.

5. Interest-rate risk: Lo-Risk Bank and Hi-Risk Bank.

40

its anticipated profit of 0.4 turns into a loss of 4.4, which it is able to withstand by writing down its capital from 8 to 3.2. Hi-Risk Bank's unexpected additional interest expense is 10.1, and its anticipated profit of 0.6 turns into a loss of 9.5. This loss wipes out Hi-Risk Bank's capital of 8, rendering Hi-Risk Bank insolvent once again.

Operational risk refers to the risk of losses associated with the operations of a bank's physical or human resources. Terrorism, or natural disasters such as floods or earthquakes, may threaten buildings or computer systems. Negligence, human error, or fraudulent behaviour on the part of individual employees, may threaten the solvency of banks.

Settlement or payments risk arises from a mismatch between the timing of payments and receipts. Banks often borrow and lend large amounts to and from each other daily in interbank markets. Interbank lending enables banks with temporary surplus liquidity to earn a return, while banks facing a temporary liquidity shortage can acquire the funds they require. Settlement in interbank markets is usually based on net positions, but if a bank incurs demands for payment in advance of its offsetting claims for settlement, it might find itself unable to meet its obligations, and its stability might be threatened. Since the gross trading volumes underlying the banks' net trading positions are very large, the collapse of one bank due to a temporary liquidity shortfall might quickly undermine the stability of other banks.

Currency risk affects banks that hold assets and liabilities denominated in different currencies, and arises when adverse movements in foreign exchange rates cause the balance sheet value of assets to decrease, or the value of liabilities to increase, or both.

Sovereign or political risk refers to risks to the profitability or feasibility of transacting banking business emanating from the decisions of sovereign governments. For example, a sovereign government might nationalize one or more banks, effectively expropriating their assets. A sovereign government might impose controls on interest rates, or on the exchange of foreign currency. A sovereign government might impose punitive taxation on banks or other financial institutions. Any of these measures might have serious effects on profitability, or the ability of banks to trade.

Chapter 3
Securitized banking

The traditional business model of banking is based on the role of the bank as financial intermediary, as described in Chapter 2. During the two or three decades that preceded the global financial crisis of 2007–9, an alternative business model evolved, which operated alongside or even supplanted traditional banking. The term 'securitized banking' has been coined to refer to this alternative business model.

The repo market, and other sources of short-term funding

An important element in the development of the securitized banking model was a growing tendency for banks to rely less heavily on deposits as a source of short-term funding, and more heavily on other sources. One such source, used widely by banks and some shadow banking institutions, is the repo (sale and repurchase) market. The bank (or any other party wishing to use the repo market to raise short-term liquid funding) sells a security (such as a government bond, corporate bond, or company share) to an investor, and agrees to repurchase the same security from the same investor at some later date, often the next day. The repurchase price is slightly higher than the sale price; and the difference is similar to an interest payment on an overnight deposit of funds. Typically the sale price is set below the value of the underlying security, giving the seller (effectively the borrower) an incentive not to default on the commitment to repurchase. If this party does default, the investor has the right to terminate the agreement and either keep or sell the security. The 'haircut' is defined as the percentage that is subtracted from the market value of the asset being used as collateral, dependent on the perceived risk associated with holding the security.

The repo market has grown enormously over the past three decades. The main advantage for the investors providing the funding is that the security serves as collateral for the transaction. The purchaser under a repo agreement (lender) can sell the security if the seller (borrower) defaults on the commitment to repurchase. In the event that the seller files for bankruptcy, without the collateral the purchaser would be just one of many creditors attempting to recover funds via bankruptcy proceedings. In traditional financial intermediation the deposits of small savers are guaranteed by government-backed deposit insurance. The latter, however, does not extend to large investors such as corporations, or shadow banking and other financial institutions. The repo market meets the needs of large investors for a market in short-term secured lending and borrowing.

Other sources of short-term funding include commercial paper (CP), a short-term promissory note issued by a large corporation with a fixed maturity, usually a maximum of nine months. CP is used by reputable corporations with high credit ratings to borrow funds over short periods, to cover items such as stocks or other current assets. CP is not backed by collateral; instead, the purchaser/investor relies upon the issuer's reputation. CP usually carries a higher yield than corporate bonds.

Asset-backed commercial paper (ABCP) is another short-term security, usually with a maturity between three and six months. When a company wishes to raise funds, it may approach a bank to issue ABCP to be purchased by investors. The ABCP, which is often issued through a Special Purpose Vehicle (SPV), may be backed by trade receivables: amounts owing to the company in payment for goods or services supplied to its customers. As the receivables are collected, the company passes the proceeds to the bank or SPV, which in turn makes repayments to the investors.

Derivatives

A derivative is a security whose value depends upon (is 'derived from') the price of one or more underlying financial securities or indices, such as shares, bonds, share indices, interest rates, commodities, or exchange rates. Derivatives can be traded on organized exchanges or over-the-counter (OTC). OTC derivatives are negotiated and traded bilaterally by the two parties to the transaction. The main types of derivative are forwards, futures, swaps, and options. Forwards are OTC agreements between two parties to undertake an exchange at a specified date in the future based on a price that is agreed today. Futures are similar to forwards, but traded on an organized exchange. Swaps commit the parties to a series of exchanges of cash flows at agreed dates in the future. Common examples are interest rate, currency, and commodity swaps. Options provide the right, but not the obligation, for a party to either buy (in the case of a call option) or sell (put option) a financial asset at a given price on, or sometimes before, a given date. Option holders are free to exercise the right to buy or sell, or to allow this contractual right to lapse. A credit derivative is a derivative whose value depends on the credit risk associated with a portfolio of loans.

Banks use derivatives as risk-management tools to hedge their exposures to adverse movements in interest rates or foreign exchange rates. Banks may also speculate, by taking a position in a derivative in the hope of profiting from a change in the price of the underlying asset. The implications of derivatives for risk are similar to those of leverage, offering investors the potential to earn enormous profits, but with a downside risk of huge losses. In 1995, for example, Barings, one of the UK's oldest investment banks, collapsed after one of its traders lost $1.3bn in derivatives trading. The OTC derivatives market is enormous in scale. According to the Bank for International Settlements (BIS), at the end of June 2014 the notional amount of outstanding OTC derivatives contracts was $691 trillion, while the gross market value stood at $17 trillion.

Securitization

Having raised short-term funding through the repo market or by other means, the bank can deploy these funds to support loans to borrowers such as house purchasers. Under a traditional banking model, the bank typically checks the borrower's credit history and ability to repay the loan. Under a securitized banking model, these functions are commonly outsourced to direct lenders such as mortgage brokers, which originate and hold loans only for very short periods, before they are sold on to banks.

The term securitization refers to the practice whereby a bank bundles a large number of loans together, and sells the package to a Structured Investment Vehicle (SIV) set up by the bank to administer the loans. The bank that either originates the loan itself, or purchases the loan from a direct lender, does not retain the loan on its balance sheet until maturity. Instead the bank receives a lump-sum cash payment in exchange for surrendering the stream of income (repayments) the loan is expected to generate. The SIV finances its acquisition of a bundle of loans by issuing structured securities, backed by the anticipated future income streams from the loans. These securities are known as asset-backed securities (ABS) or, where the underlying loans are mortgages on residential property, mortgage-backed securities (MBS). The SIV hires the services of an underwriter, typically an investment bank, to assume responsibility for designing, marketing, and selling the ABS to investors. In exchange for their lump-sum investment in acquiring the ABS, the investors receive regular payments from the income streams emanating from the underlying loans. Although MBS represent the largest single component of the market for ABS, any asset or activity that is expected to generate a future income stream can be securitized in a similar manner. For example, student loans and credit-card fees and interest payments have also been securitized, resulting in the creation of new ABS.

In the case of MBS, especially in the US where many small banks trade solely in their own local areas, geographical diversification was believed to be one of the main advantages of securitization, prior to the global financial crisis. A small bank that had originated mortgages locally and retained these mortgages on its own balance sheet would be vulnerable to a local property market collapse. By bundling the mortgages together with many others secured against properties in different locations, the investors at the end of the securitization chain benefit from a geographical diversification effect, which largely insulates them from the risk of any localized property market collapse. Of course, this geographical diversification benefit would be negated by a nationwide collapse in property prices.

In many ways, the practices employed by SIVs and underwriters to structure MBS (and ABS in general) tended to magnify rather than reduce risk in the financial system. A key risk-enhancing design feature of MBS was the practice of tranching, whereby several categories of securities were created in each securitization issue, with different terms concerning the absorption of losses resulting from defaults on the underlying portfolio of mortgages. In a highly simplified and stylized example, suppose a pool of 2,500 one-year mortgages with an average value of $200,000 and an anticipated annual default rate of 2 per cent, is to be securitized. A typical securitization might create a junior tranche, responsible for absorbing the first 10 per cent of any losses arising from defaults; a mezzanine tranche, responsible for absorbing the next 5 per cent of default losses; and a senior tranche, responsible for absorbing any default losses beyond the first 15 per cent

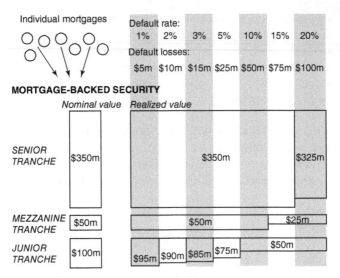

Individual mortgages

	Default rate:						
	1%	2%	3%	5%	10%	15%	20%
	Default losses:						
	$5m	$10m	$15m	$25m	$50m	$75m	$100m

MORTGAGE-BACKED SECURITY

Nominal value   Realized value

	Nominal value	Realized value
SENIOR TRANCHE	$350m	$350m ... $325m
MEZZANINE TRANCHE	$50m	$50m ... $25m
JUNIOR TRANCHE	$100m	$95m $90m $85m $75m $50m

6. **Tranching of a mortgage-backed security.**

covered by the junior and mezzanine tranches. Figure 6 illustrates the structure of the MBS, and examines the implications of various rates of default loss for the realized values of the junior, mezzanine, and senior tranches.

The nominal value of the junior tranche might be $100m; but because anticipated default losses are equivalent to 2 per cent of the entire portfolio, amounting to $10m, the junior tranche is sold to investors at a discount to the nominal value. The discount required by investors to purchase the junior tranche is at least 10 per cent, reducing the sale price to $90m, factoring in $10m of anticipated losses. In practice the discount might be even larger, depending on the market's assessment of the risk that the default rate will turn out to be higher (perhaps substantially higher) than 2 per cent. The risk borne by the purchasers of the junior tranche is magnified by the structure of the MBS: if the default losses are

1 per cent of the entire pool of mortgages ($5m), the junior tranche is worth $95m, but if the losses are 3 per cent ($15m) the junior tranche is worth only $85m. A swing of 1 per cent in the default rate in either direction causes a swing of 5.5 per cent in the realized value of the junior tranche, relative to its $90m value when the default rate is 2 per cent.

Default losses affect holders of the mezzanine tranche if the default rate on the entire pool of mortgages exceeds 10 per cent. Under normal property market conditions prevalent before the global financial crisis, most market participants would have assigned a negligibly small probability to this outcome. The mezzanine tranche would have been sold to investors at a price very close to its nominal value, and would likely have been assigned the highest possible, risk-free, credit rating. Likewise the senior tranche would have sold at its nominal value and would have been rated risk-free.

The practice of tranching not only magnified risk, but also created complexity and opacity. Did investors in the various tranches of MBS fully understand the structure of their investments and the risks they were running? Risk, complexity, and opacity were further increased, however, by other innovations in the design of structured securities and derivatives prior to the global financial crisis. Extending the previous example, the junior tranches from five separate MBS issues could be bundled together and subject to further tranching, to create a new security called a collateralized debt obligation (CDO), a type of credit derivative. In the example, the CDO would have a nominal value of $500m, broken down into five equal-sized tranches each with nominal value $100m. Expected default losses, if the default rate on the five underlying bundles of mortgages is 2 per cent, are $50m ($5 × $10m). The lowest tranche of the CDO might be made responsible for absorbing the first 4 per cent ($100m) of default losses arising from defaults across all five bundles of mortgages. The next tranche might be made responsible for absorbing the next 4 per cent of default losses, and so on. As before, most of the default risk appears to be contained within the lowest tranche. Provided the default rate on the underlying pool is not more than 4 per cent (twice the expected rate), default losses are borne solely by holders of the lowest tranche. The lowest tranche sells at a large discount to its nominal value and attracts a low credit rating; but the remaining four tranches sell close to their nominal values and attract high credit ratings.

Whereas formerly all five junior tranches of MBS, with combined nominal value $500m, were all regarded as high risk, four of the five tranches of the CDO, with nominal value $400m, are now regarded as low risk and trade close to their nominal value. The creation of the CDO appears to have substantially reduced the risk associated with 80 per cent of the MBS. During the global financial crisis, however, mortgage loan defaults occurred on a scale that caused substantial losses among CDO tranches that had originally been rated as very low risk (see Chapter 6).

Figure 7 shows a schematic representation of the securitized banking business model. The upper part of the figure is similar to the traditional banking business model, in which the bank acts as an intermediary between depositors and borrowers. The lower part of the figure shows the main elements of the securitized banking model, with pools of mortgages passed from the bank to its SIV and packaged into an MBS, which are either sold direct to investors, or repackaged into a CDO prior to sale to investors. The bank may also raise short-term finance through repo markets or selling an ABCP.

Another type of credit derivative, the credit default swap (CDS), was a financial innovation of the years preceding the global financial crisis, whose uses or misuses were later heavily implicated among the causes of the crisis. A CDS is an insurance contract which insures the buyer against losses arising from default on the part of the issuer of a security. The security could be a government bond, a corporate bond, an ABS, or a CDO. The

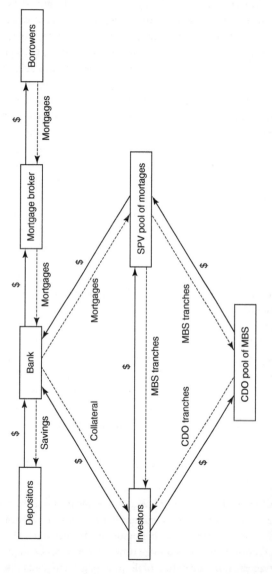

Note: Thick arrows denote cash flows. Dotted arrows denote transfer of corresponding assets/liabilities.

7. **The securitized banking business model.**

buyer of the CDS (the insured) pays a regular premium, known as the CDS spread, to the seller of the CDS (the insurer) until the maturity of the underlying security or until the security defaults. In the event that the security defaults, the seller of the CDS pays the buyer an amount that covers the loss caused by the default.

Originally created to enable bondholders to hedge against possible losses from bond defaults, in other words to mitigate risk, CDS markets grew explosively during the 2000s. For 2015, the Bank for International Settlements (BIS) reports an aggregate gross market value of all CDS contracts of $453bn. Much of the early growth in CDS markets was fuelled by investors taking a speculative position on the prospect of a corporate default, often without any 'insurable interest' in the form of holdings of the company's bonds. Both the buyer and the seller of the CDS contract, known as the CDS counterparties, are exposed to risk in the sense that the outcome of the CDS transaction is uncertain at the outset: there is a high probability that there is no default and the buyer pays a small sum to the seller; and a low probability that there is a default and the seller pays a large sum to the buyer. At the height of the global financial crisis, the systemic risk (the risk to the stability of the entire financial system) posed by CDS was ruthlessly exposed: what happens if the seller (insurer) becomes insolvent and cannot pay out if the underlying security defaults? The default of one CDS counterparty through insolvency could render many others insolvent, owing to their dependence on receiving payouts from the initial defaulter.

The shadow banking system and securitized banking

The shadow banking system plays a major role in the securitized banking model, alongside investment banks and some commercial banks. In the securitized banking model the traditional intermediation function is broken down into a series of stages, facilitating the transformation of illiquid long-term loans into short-term securities. Shadow banking activity draws upon collateralized funding such as repo, as well as non-collateralized short-term commercial paper (CP), and asset-backed commercial paper (ABCP).

The activities of shadow banking entities can enhance liquidity and spread risk. For example, securitization enables illiquid assets such as mortgages to be traded in liquid markets for MBS. However, many shadow banking institutions are highly leveraged and opaque, and escape regulatory and supervisory scrutiny because they are not licensed as banks. Deposits with shadow banking institutions are not covered by government deposit insurance, or central bank lender-of-last-resort support. Efforts to strengthen the regulation of traditional banking might prove counterproductive if they encourage the migration of risky activities to the unregulated shadow banking sector. Shadow banking poses risks for financial stability, in view of the interconnectedness of traditional banks and shadow banking institutions. Banks are often major investors in securities created by shadow banking institutions, and banks often provide credit guarantees to shadow banking institutions. Therefore any instability in the shadow banking system is likely to impact directly upon the stability of traditional banks.

Chapter 4

The central bank and the conduct of monetary policy

In most countries, the central bank is the bank that manages the country's money supply and interest rates. Most central banks hold a monopoly over printing the national currency, and most have supervisory or regulatory responsibilities for overseeing the banking industry. One exception is the European Central Bank (ECB), which delegates responsibility for the supervision and regulation of smaller banks within the Eurozone to national level. The central bank typically performs a dual role, operating as the government's banker, and as banker to the rest of the banking system.

The role of the central bank

In its capacity as the government's banker, the central bank manages the government's finances, and takes responsibility for money and credit creation and the implementation of monetary policy. Monetary policy involves influencing the supply and demand for money and credit, and the level of interest rates. The central bank exerts influence in several ways: by trading securities, such as government or corporate bonds; by trading foreign currencies in foreign exchange markets; and by direct lending to commercial banks. If the central bank feels the economy is growing too fast, and inflation is at risk of increasing, the conventional policy response is to raise interest rates, so as to dampen the demand for borrowing by firms and consumers, reducing expenditure on goods and services throughout the economy. Conversely, if the economy is growing too slowly, and inflation is low or perhaps even at risk of turning negative (deflation), interest rates may be lowered to stimulate demand for borrowing and boost expenditure on goods and services.

The government might assign to the central bank responsibilities for some or all of the following policy objectives: maintaining low and stable inflation, maintaining high and stable economic growth, and maintaining high employment, interest rate stability, exchange rate stability, and financial market stability. While politicians may dictate and be held accountable for the policy objectives assigned to the central bank, in recent decades the principle of operational independence, meaning no political interference in operational matters, has gained acceptance as a constitutional feature of many central banks around the world. The principle of independence means the central bank should exercise control over its own funding, and should take decisions that cannot be overridden or reversed by politicians. Commonly, monetary policy decisions are taken by committees, whose membership may include senior central bank executives, and independent external members such as banking industry executives or academics specializing in monetary economics or macroeconomics. In many central banks committee decisions are taken transparently, with minutes of committee meetings or voting patterns (numbers of committee members voting for and against a motion to raise or lower interest rates, for example) published.

In its role as banker to the rest of the banking system, the central bank provides banking services to other banks. All commercial banks are required by law to maintain deposits, known as reserves, at the central bank. Commercial banks can obtain the funds needed to service their day-to-day operations either routinely, by borrowing from the central bank in the course of normal trading, or in the case of a bank encountering financial difficulties, through emergency borrowing from the central bank in its capacity as lender of last resort. The central bank also manages the interbank payments network; and performs a supervisory role by overseeing the activities of individual banks, in pursuit of the objective of financial stability.

Central banks in the UK, EU, and US

The Bank of England, the central bank of the United Kingdom, was shareholder-owned until the Bank was nationalized in 1946. In 1997 an incoming Labour government announced that the Bank of England would be granted operational independence in determining monetary policy; independence was implemented in 1998. The Bank's Monetary Policy Committee (MPC) is responsible for the management of monetary policy. The MPC comprises the governor, two deputy governors, two of the Bank's executive directors, and four other members appointed by the Chancellor of the Exchequer. The MPC is responsible for setting the Bank of England base rate, the interest rate at which the Bank lends short-term funds to commercial banks, on a monthly basis. In setting the base rate, the MPC is required to pursue an inflation target determined by the government, originally 2½ per cent on a retail price index inflation measure, but adjusted to 2 per cent on an alternative consumer price index measure in 2003.

The European Central Bank (ECB) was set up in 1998 to act as the central bank to the Eurozone, which (currently) comprises eighteen of the twenty-eight European Union (EU) member states. The central banks of the twenty-eight member states are the owners of the ECB's capital. The ECB's Executive Board, comprising the President, Vice President, and four other members appointed by the heads of government of EU member states, is responsible for the implementation of monetary policy. The Governing Council, comprising the six members of the Executive Board and the governors of the eighteen Eurozone member countries' central banks, is the main decision-making body. The ECB pursues a single objective of price stability, defined as inflation within the Eurozone close to, but below, 2 per cent on a harmonized consumer price index measure. In contrast to many other central banks, the ECB is prohibited from directly purchasing bonds issued by Eurozone member governments as a means of exerting downward pressure on interest rates, a practice known as monetary financing. In recent years, however, the ECB has traded heavily in secondary markets for Eurozone government debt.

In the US the Federal Reserve System was created in 1913, and comprises twelve regional Federal Reserve Banks, of which the largest and most important is the Federal Reserve Bank of New York. The Federal Reserve Banks are federally chartered non-profit banks, owned privately by the commercial banks in their regions that are members of the Federal Reserve System. All federally-chartered banks and some state-chartered banks are members. The Federal Reserve System is overseen by the Federal Reserve Board of Governors, tasked (by Congress) with the promotion of high employment, stable prices, and moderate long-term interest rates. The Federal Open Market Committee (FOMC) is responsible for the conduct of monetary and interest rate policy.

The central bank's balance sheet

A central bank's main instruments for influencing the volumes of money and credit in circulation throughout the economy operate by expanding or contracting the size of its own balance sheet. Table 3 shows the main entries on the assets and liabilities sides of the central bank's balance sheet.

The liabilities recorded in the central bank's balance sheet are the sources of the funds used by the central bank to finance its trading activities, and the central bank's capital (net worth). Currency issued or deposits created by the central bank, and held outside

Table 3 Elements of a central bank's balance sheet

Assets	Liabilities
Securities	Currency held by non-bank public
Foreign exchange reserves	Government deposits
Loans	Reserves: commercial bank deposits, and currency held by commercial banks
	Total liabilities
	Capital/net worth (= Total assets *minus* Total liabilities)
Total assets	**Total liabilities and capital**

the banking system, are a source of funding, and are therefore treated as a liability.

Government deposits at the central bank arise from the government's need to operate an account which receives government revenues, primarily from taxation, and from which payments are made for government purchases.

Reserves comprise deposits made by commercial banks at the central bank, and currency held by commercial banks in their own vaults. Commercial bank deposits at the central bank can be withdrawn on demand, and these deposits, together with the cash held by the commercial banks in their own vaults, define the total funds available to the commercial banks to satisfy their depositors' demands for withdrawals. In order to maintain depositor confidence in the banking system, some countries' central banks stipulate a minimum reserve requirement, whereby each commercial bank must maintain reserves equivalent to a specified percentage of its deposits. In countries without any statutory minimum reserve requirement, commercial banks still maintain reserves to demonstrate they have sufficient liquidity to meet their day-to-day demand for withdrawals by depositors.

On the liabilities side of the central bank's balance sheet, the sum of currency held by the non-bank public and commercial banks' reserves (including their own currency holdings) is known as the monetary base.

On the assets side of the central bank's balance sheet, operating along similar lines to any other bank, the central bank employs the funds it raises from its depositors and from other sources to grant loans, and purchase other assets.

Securities are the largest item on the assets side of most central banks' balance sheets. Before the global financial crisis, the majority of the securities held by central banks were government bonds, issued by the home-country government. During the crisis, many central banks attempted to restore confidence in financial markets through large-scale purchases of other, riskier securities, such as corporate bonds and MBS (mortgage-backed securities).

Foreign exchange reserves are the central bank's holdings of foreign currencies, including bonds issued by other governments and denominated in foreign currency units. A country's exports and its inflows of capital investment create a demand at the central bank for conversion of foreign currency units into domestic currency, causing the central bank's foreign currency reserves to accumulate. Conversely, imports and outflows of capital investment create a demand for conversion of domestic currency units into foreign currency, depleting foreign currency reserves. Central banks may intervene directly in the foreign exchange markets in an effort to influence or stabilize foreign exchange rates, the market prices at which currency pairs can be converted.

Traditionally commercial banks were the main recipients of central bank loans. During the global financial crisis, however, some central banks loaned funds, on a large scale, direct to non-financial companies, in an attempt to compensate for the efforts of many banks to reduce their loans portfolios by cutting back on new lending. Discount loans are granted routinely to commercial banks that need short-term funding. Typically the borrowing bank must demonstrate, by posting collateral, that it qualifies for a central bank loan at the standard rate of interest, known as the discount rate. Distressed banks that fail to qualify to borrow at the discount rate, and are unable to raise funds elsewhere, may apply for an emergency central bank loan at a higher interest rate. In acting in its lender-of-last-resort capacity, the central bank needs to ascertain that the distressed bank is fundamentally secure, and that the loan will assist the bank in progressing on a pathway towards recovery.

The International Monetary Fund

The International Monetary Fund (IMF), headquartered in New York, was originally formed in 1945 to promote the international coordination and oversight of monetary policy, provide loans to countries experiencing balance of payments deficits that would threaten to wipe out their foreign exchange reserves, and reconstruct the international payments system following the Great Depression of the 1930s and the Second World War. Currently 188 member countries contribute funds on a quota system to a pool, from which loans can be drawn by member countries experiencing balance of payments difficulties, via their central banks. The rationale for an emergency borrowing facility for countries is that in its absence, countries facing depletion of their foreign exchange reserves might need to adopt extreme and highly disruptive deflationary measures to curb a balance of payments deficit, and avoid defaulting on their commitments to international creditors. Alternatively, deficit countries might simply choose to default. The availability of an emergency borrowing facility helps promote international financial stability. Borrowing from the IMF is usually made conditional on the adoption of policy measures aimed at correcting any underlying macroeconomic imbalances deemed to have contributed to or caused the balance of payments deficit. The IMF has at times been criticized for imposing harsh conditionality on access to emergency funding.

The conduct of monetary policy

A central bank's responsibility for the implementation of monetary policy derives from the fact that, uniquely among all banks, as well as other financial institutions and non-financial companies, the central bank exercises direct control over the size and composition of its own balance sheet.

Open market operations (OMO) involve the central bank in buying or selling securities in the open market. The securities traded in an OMO transaction are usually government bonds, or other types of fixed-interest security. Typically the central bank engages in OMO by trading securities with commercial banks. Suppose the central bank purchases securities worth £100 in the open market, and the seller is Bank A. Ownership of the securities is transferred from Bank A to the central bank; and Bank A's account at the central bank, containing Bank A's reserves, is credited with £100 in payment for the securities. The adjustments to the balance sheets of Bank A and the central bank are summarized in Table 4.

Table 4 **Open market operations, and commercial bank and central bank balance sheets**

Bank A		Central bank	
Assets	**Liabilities**	**Assets**	**Liabilities**
Securities −100		Securities +100	Reserves +100
Reserves +100			

As a result of this OMO transaction, Bank A undergoes a change in the composition of its balance sheet on the assets side: its securities portfolio is depleted by £100, but this is compensated by an increase in its reserves (deposits with the central bank) of £100. The central bank, meanwhile, undergoes an expansion of its balance sheet: on the assets side, its securities portfolio is increased by £100; and on the liabilities side reserves (deposits obtained from commercial banks) increase by £100.

Foreign exchange intervention, which involves the central bank in buying or selling foreign currency on the foreign exchange (FX) markets, also affects the central bank's balance sheet. The central bank might trade either in currency (banknotes), or in bonds issued by foreign governments and denominated in foreign currency units. Suppose the central bank purchases currency worth £100 from Bank A. The currency is transferred from Bank A to the central bank; and Bank A's account at the central bank is credited with £100 in payment for the currency. As in the OMO example, the central bank undergoes an expansion of its balance sheet: on the assets side, its foreign exchange reserves are increased by £100; and on the liabilities side reserves (deposits obtained from commercial banks) are increased by £100.

Lending to commercial banks has a similar effect on the central bank's balance sheet. Suppose the central bank lends £100 to Bank A, which wishes to borrow. This transaction is implemented by crediting Bank A's account at the central bank with £100. The central bank undergoes an expansion of its balance sheet: the loan to Bank A is an asset valued at £100; but on the liabilities side reserves (deposits obtained from commercial banks) also increase by £100.

In practice, foreign exchange intervention and direct lending to commercial banks are used less commonly than OMO in the day-to-day operation of monetary policy. In many countries foreign exchange intervention is targeted primarily at management of the exchange rate. Direct lending by the central bank to commercial banks, known as discount lending, is usually small except in times of crisis, when banks may have no option other than to borrow from the central bank.

The deposit expansion multiplier

How does a change in the size of the central bank's balance sheet translate into a change in the money supply, the total quantity of money in circulation throughout the economy? Money supply definitions vary between countries, but generally speaking official monetary aggregates can be classified as either narrow or broad. The narrow money supply, also known as the monetary base, comprises cash held by the non-bank public and commercial banks' reserves (cash in the banks' vaults, and their deposits with the central bank). Broad money supply measures include a wider range of liquid financial securities and bank deposits.

How does an increase in the size of the liabilities on the central bank's balance sheet, or the narrow money supply, affect the broad money supply? A mechanical answer to this question refers to the 'deposit expansion multiplier'. Few economists would adhere to the deposit expansion multiplier as a literal description of how monetary policy operates; but the following example nevertheless illustrates how the banking system contributes to the creation of money.

Suppose all commercial banks aim to maintain reserves (deposits with the central bank or cash in vaults) equivalent to 10 per cent of their total deposits. Figure 8 shows that when the central bank buys securities from Bank A via OMO, Bank A's reserves at the central bank increase, even though there is no change in Bank A's deposits. Bank A is suddenly holding reserves above the targeted 10 per cent of its deposits. Bank A may react to the increase in its reserves by granting new loans, because it earns a higher rate of interest on its lending than the rate paid by the central bank on reserves. Bank A grants a loan of £100 to one of its customers, by crediting the customer's account. Bank A's reserves at the central

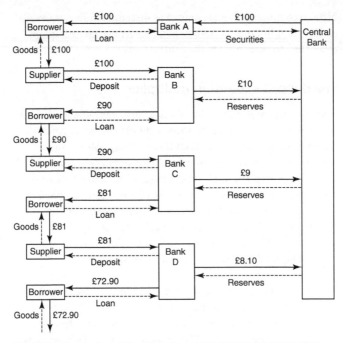

Note: Thick arrows denote cash flows. Dotted arrows denote transfer of corresponding assets/liabilities.

8. The deposit expansion multiplier.

bank are reduced by the same amount. The customer then spends the £100 loan, either by writing a cheque or transferring electronically into the account of a supplier of goods or services.

Suppose the supplier's bank account is with Bank B. Bank B finds its deposits have increased by £100, and must decide how to deploy this additional funding. Bank B needs to increase its reserves at the central bank by £10 in line with the £100 increase in its deposits to maintain the 10 per cent target. The remaining £90 is available to Bank B to grant a further loan. The borrower spends the £90 loan, which is transferred into the account of another supplier of goods or services.

Suppose this supplier's bank account is with Bank C. Bank C finds its deposits have increased by £90, and must decide how to deploy this additional funding. Bank C needs to increase its reserves at the central bank by £9 to maintain the 10 per cent target. The remaining £81 is available to Bank C to grant a further loan. The process of deposit expansion continues indefinitely, but with successively smaller and smaller loans being granted on each round, as shown in Figure 8.

All of the new bank deposits created through this process contribute to the broad money supply. The overall increase in the broad money supply is as follows:

$$£100 + £90 + £81 + £72.90 + £65.61 + £59.05\ldots = £1000$$

The deposit expansion multiplier in this example is 10: an initial £100 expansion of the narrow money supply effected via OMO leads to a £1000 expansion of the broad money supply. In reality the impact on the broad money supply may be less predictable than this example suggests. Two other factors may enter the picture, in a way that reduces the deposit expansion multiplier, as follows.

First, in the example, it is assumed that each bank prefers lending to holding reserves above the 10 per cent target at the central bank, because it earns more interest on its lending than it earns on its reserves. However, lending is risky, and at times banks may opt for safety by increasing their reserves rather than lending the maximum amounts their balance sheets could support. As the deposit expansion process gets underway, if some of the additional deposits are channelled into accumulating reserves, the deposit expansion multiplier is reduced.

Second, if the bank customers who are the borrowers of the additional loans granted, or the suppliers of the goods and services purchased using borrowed money, decide to hold part of the additional monies they receive in the form of cash, rather than bank deposits, the process of deposit expansion is impeded. In the example, it is assumed that each additional loan ends up as a deposit with another bank, and is used subsequently to support further lending. If part of the additional lending is held by the general public in cash, the deposit expansion multiplier is reduced.

Interest rate targeting

In principle, the central bank's use of OMO, foreign exchange intervention, and direct lending to commercial banks, might allow direct control over narrow money, and indirect control over broad money via the deposit expansion multiplier. In practice, however, the deposit expansion multiplier has turned out to be too unstable for these types of operation to serve as the basis for the conduct of monetary policy. Some central banks, including the Bank of England and the central banks of Sweden, Australia, and New Zealand, do not stipulate any minimum reserve requirement; instead they rely on other tools, such as capital requirements, to constrain bank lending. Even those central banks that do stipulate reserve requirements, such as the Federal Reserve and the ECB, do not view the adjustment of these requirements as a practical tool for the implementation of monetary policy. Instead, most central banks set a target for the market interest rate on overnight interbank lending, and seek to manipulate the total quantity of reserves, primarily through OMO, so that the actual interbank lending rate, determined in the market in which banks lend and borrow funds to and from each other, corresponds closely to the target rate. The discount rate is a higher rate for central bank lending to banks that cannot meet their funding requirements on the interbank market. The deposit rate is a lower rate payable on reserves. The discount rate and the deposit rate place a ceiling and a floor, respectively, on the market interbank rate.

Figure 9 provides a diagrammatic representation of demand and supply in the market for interbank lending. The downward-sloping line is the demand for borrowed funds shown as a function of the interest rate: the lower the interest rate, the higher is the demand to borrow funds. The central bank decides its target for the interbank lending rate, estimates the level of demand at this target rate, and then supplies this quantity of reserves through its OMO. This makes the supply of reserves vertical at the estimated level of demand. The supply becomes horizontal at the discount rate, because the central bank is willing to meet requests from any eligible bank to borrow funds at this rate; and the demand is horizontal at the deposit rate because banks would be willing to borrow any amount if they are guaranteed that the same rate can be earned on reserves deposited with the central bank.

As a guide for interest rate targeting, the Taylor Rule, attributed to John Taylor of Stanford University following research published in 1993, was highly influential, especially before the global financial crisis. The Taylor Rule states that when inflation is above its target, or when actual output is above potential output causing inflationary pressures to build, the target interbank lending rate

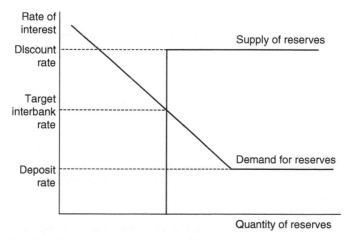

9. **Demand and supply for interbank lending.**

should be raised above the level consistent with the inflation target and full employment. Conversely when inflation is below its target, or when actual output is below potential output resulting in high unemployment, the target interbank lending rate should be lowered below the level consistent with the inflation target and full employment. Although the US Federal Reserve never adopted the Taylor Rule explicitly, several empirical studies have shown that the formula provides an accurate description of the conduct of US monetary policy for much of the 1990s and early 2000s. In many other countries as well, interest rate targeting became the favoured approach for steering monetary policy. Targeting the money supply, practised widely during the 1980s, was ultimately discredited due to the lack of any clear relationship between targeted monetary aggregates and goals such as low and stable inflation. Direct targeting of inflation, practised widely during the 1990s, was disadvantaged by uncertain time-lags, and a tendency for a sole emphasis on stable inflation to heighten instability in output and unemployment.

Quantitative easing and forward guidance

The upheavals of 2007–9 demonstrated starkly that circumstances can arise under which conventional tools for the implementation of monetary policy are incapable of providing the kind of stimulus required to avert the most damaging economic consequences of a financial crisis. One difficulty with interest rate targeting arises if the target rate of interest falls below zero. Banks may not choose to lend to other banks for negative interest; instead, they may prefer to hoard cash and earn a zero return. Therefore the Taylor Rule fails to provide useful guidance for monetary policy in cases where a target interest rate of zero yields insufficient economic stimulus.

Another difficulty arises when financial markets become impaired owing to a general loss of confidence. For example, at the height of the global financial crisis following the collapse of the Lehman Brothers investment bank in September 2008, volumes of lending on interbank markets plummeted, as banks lost confidence in each others' ability to repay monies borrowed. Commercial banks seeking to restore their capital-to-assets ratios after writing off delinquent loans or writing down the value of other assets cut back aggressively on their lending to small businesses and other borrowers. These developments had major consequences for the effectiveness of monetary policy conducted using mechanisms such as interest rate targeting.

Perhaps the best-known 'unconventional' monetary policy tool, used extensively since the crisis, is quantitative easing (QE). This refers to a central bank policy of purchasing securities from banks and other financial institutions, and supplying reserves beyond the quantity required to reduce the target policy interest rate to zero. A policy of QE is illustrated in Figure 10. The securities purchased may include government bonds, or other riskier securities such as bonds issued by private companies, or mortgage-backed securities (MBS).

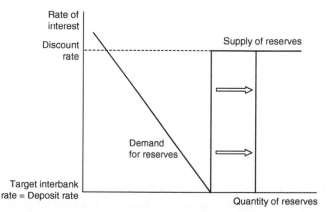

10. **Effect of quantitative easing on the market for interbank lending.**

There are several channels through which a QE programme might influence the level of economic activity. First, the additional reserves supplied to the banking system could provide the foundation for increased bank lending to the private sector, through the deposit expansion multiplier. Second, banks that sell long-term securities to the central bank may be keen to use the proceeds to lend long-term, in order to maintain a desired ratio between short-term and long-term assets on their balance sheets. Third, QE could influence economic activity through its effect on the demand for long-term borrowing. By increasing the demand for long-dated securities, the prices of these securities are increased, placing downward pressure on long-term interest rates. This may make firms more willing to borrow, increasing the level of economic activity. Finally, the large-scale purchase of securities by the central bank may help restore confidence to impaired financial markets.

Closely related to QE but conceptually distinct is the policy of credit easing, which involves buying longer-term or high-risk securities through OMO, and selling shorter-term or low-risk securities. Whereas QE focuses on the expansion of the total quantity of reserves on the liabilities side of the central bank's balance sheet, credit easing focuses on changing the composition of the portfolio of securities recorded on the assets side of the balance sheet, without affecting the reserves that can be used by the commercial banks to support lending. Unlike QE, therefore, credit easing cannot be construed as tantamount to a central bank policy of 'printing money'. Instead, the purchase of long-dated government or corporate bonds should increase the demand for these securities, raising their prices, lowering long-term interest rates, and adjusting the relative quantities of credit available for short-term and long-term bank lending in favour of the latter.

Another 'unconventional' monetary policy tool is forward guidance, whereby the central bank makes a verbal commitment as to how it will conduct monetary or interest rate policy in the future. Such a commitment could be made for a specific period, or it could be open-ended. A commitment could be unconditional, or conditional on economic conditions. For example, a central bank could commit not to raise short-term interest rates while the unemployment rate remains above 7 per cent, or while the rate of inflation remains below 3 per cent. The central bank's aim in issuing forward guidance is to gain influence over long-term interest rates via its control over short-term rates. Suppose the central bank wishes to lower the interest rate to 1 per cent on borrowing with a maturity of three years. It can do so by pledging to maintain the (overnight) interbank lending rate at 1 per cent for at least three years. The rate for borrowing with a three-year maturity should reflect the market's expectations of the average value of the interbank rate over a three-year period. If the central bank's commitment is believed, the three-year rate should adjust to the target value of 1 per cent.

Chapter 5

Regulation and supervision of the banking industry

As financial intermediaries, commercial banks use liquid liabilities (bank deposits) to finance illiquid assets (bank loans). Banks hold only a small proportion of their assets in the form of reserves, and cannot cope if all depositors demand the return of their funds simultaneously. Together with leverage, this makes banks inherently fragile, and creates the potential for one distressed bank to cause a loss of confidence in others. Regulation and supervision of the banking industry aims to protect individual banks, and the financial system as a whole, from the possibility of collapse.

Causes of bank runs

For the most part, banks have become expert in managing their assets and liabilities so that they can meet their day-to-day commitments to their depositors and other customers. However, if a bank fails to perform to the satisfaction of its depositors, their demands to withdraw their deposits may escalate. Few depositors have the knowledge or technical capability to form a reliable judgement of the quality of a bank's assets portfolio. Especially during times when confidence in the stability of the financial system is fragile, depositors who cannot assess the risks each bank is running in its lending practices may assume the worst and seek to withdraw their deposits. In an extreme case the bank could experience a run, as customers lose confidence in the soundness of the bank, and queues build outside high-street branches.

If customers who have withdrawn funds from a failing bank simply deposit these funds in other healthy banks, the failure of one bank might pose little or no danger for the stability of the financial system. However, a loss of depositor confidence in one bank can easily undermine confidence in the soundness of other banks, a problem known as contagion. A situation where the failure of one poorly managed bank creates a loss of confidence in other well-managed banks is an example of what economists term a negative externality. A negative externality arises whenever an economic activity imposes an uncompensated cost upon someone who is not a party to the original activity. Banking crises impact on financial stability, and on the wider economy. During a crisis that causes banks to cut back on lending, perhaps in order to reduce leverage, or restore capital to some desired level relative to assets, less credit becomes available to support enterprise and investment throughout the wider economy. Credit rationing, when viable investment projects cannot obtain funding, may have damaging consequences for output, employment, and household incomes.

Bank runs have occurred periodically throughout history. A succession of bank runs between 1930 and 1932 in the US, as the Great Depression took hold, is a prominent example. Even in modern times bank runs can occur, as was demonstrated by the collapse of the UK bank Northern Rock in 2007. Northern Rock had converted from a building society to a bank in 1997, and subsequently became a major mortgage lender. Its reported assets grew from £15.8bn in 1997 to £101bn in 2006. Much of this growth in assets was funded by short-term borrowing, rather than deposits. Many of the loans were securitized and sold to investors via a Special Purpose Vehicle (SPV), releasing capital to support further growth in lending. When the interbank markets seized up in August 2007, Northern Rock was unable to continue rolling over its funding, triggering a run on deposits (Figure 11).

11. The run on Northern Rock.

In today's sophisticated financial system, a loss of confidence in the soundness of a financial institution can arise through channels other than queues of anxious retail customers demanding to close their current or deposit accounts. A 'fire sale' refers to a situation in which a bank has insufficient cash (or other highly liquid assets) to meet the demands of its depositors for withdrawals, and is forced to sell longer-term assets, hurriedly and therefore at discounted prices, in order to raise the cash it requires. Such asset fire sales may jeopardize the solvency of the bank concerned, and other banks that are forced to mark down the valuations of similar assets on their balance sheets. When one bank takes steps to shrink its balance sheet by reducing short-term lending to other banks, these banks may also experience funding difficulties, forcing them in turn to shrink their balance sheets as interbank lending and borrowing dries up. Banks reliant on interbank markets to meet their short-term funding needs suddenly find the liquidity they require is no longer available, creating the conditions for a loss of depositor confidence.

Regulatory authorities

The potential for one poorly managed bank to damage confidence in the entire banking system creates a powerful justification for the supervision and regulation of individual banks, and the banking industry as a whole. A poorly managed hairdresser poses little or no threat to the financial viability of hairdressers in general, or to wider economic performance. Consequently in most countries hairdressers are not subject to any intrusive regulatory regime. By contrast, a poorly managed bank threatens the viability of other banks, the stability of the financial system, and the health of the economy. In most countries, elaborate arrangements have evolved for the close supervision and regulation of banks. Regulation refers to the rules for the conduct of banking business that are enshrined in legislation, or passed down by government agencies tasked with monitoring the financial system. Supervision refers to the oversight and enforcement (via sanctions if necessary) of regulation, by government agencies.

US banks may be chartered by their home state, or at federal level. The Office of the Comptroller of the Currency (OCC) regulates banks with a federal charter. The Board of Governors of the Federal Reserve System regulates state-chartered banks that are members of the Federal Reserve System, while the Federal Deposit Insurance Corporation (FDIC) regulates non-member state-chartered banks. Since the Dodd–Frank Act 2010, Savings and Loan (S&L) associations have been regulated by the OCC, FDIC, and the Federal Reserve. All banks are federally insured, and subject to rules laid down by the FDIC. Before the global financial crisis there were three advisory committees for the regulation of individual financial services providers in the EU, but no regulatory body responsible for ensuring the stability of the financial system. In February 2009 the de Larosière Report recommended that the supervisory architecture be replaced with a European System of Financial Supervision (ESFS).

Until 2012 the Financial Services Authority (FSA) was responsible for the regulation and supervision of banks and other financial institutions in the UK. In 2012 responsibilities were transferred to the Bank of England. Within the Bank of England, the Prudential Regulation Authority (PRA) is responsible for the regulation and supervision of banks, insurance, and large investment firms. The Financial Conduct Authority (FCA) sits outside the Bank of England, and takes responsibility for competition, prevention of market abuses, and consumer protection. The FCA is responsible for the regulation of asset managers, hedge funds, independent financial advisers, and smaller-sized broker-dealers. The Financial Policy Committee (FPC) of the Bank of England is responsible for monitoring, and intervening if necessary, to ensure financial stability.

Banking licenses

Under most jurisdictions the holding of a banking license is a legal prerequisite for the conduct of fundamental banking activities, such as accepting deposits from the general public. In the UK, for example, the PRA and the FCA are jointly responsible for the scrutiny of license applications. According to FCA guidelines, applicants are required to answer the following questions: Who is the applicant and what kind of entity will it be? Who are the owners and/or major capital investors and what is their country of origin? How advanced or developed is the applicant's proposition? Is the applicant part of a larger group? What is the proposed structure of the board and senior management? Applicants must also provide: a summary of the business plan including financial projections; details of the products/services, target markets, delivery channels, pricing policy, and the corresponding regulated activities that will be applied for; the applicant's funding model; market research into competitive advantage and the viability of the business; the expected scale of operations with anticipated staffing levels; and details of key outsourcing arrangements.

The government safety net

Direct government involvement in the operation of the banking and financial systems, intended to enhance financial stability, takes several forms. The lender of last resort function refers to a central bank policy of lending short-term funds to banks that are fundamentally solvent, but unable to borrow from other sources the funds required to meet the day-to-day demands of their depositors for withdrawals. Central bank lending to a bank experiencing liquidity problems usually takes place at a penal rate of interest, higher than the discount rate. The global financial crisis exposed a fundamental problem with the lender-of-last-resort concept. Suppose the secondary markets for the purchase and sale of the securities and loans held by banks as assets have ceased to function, owing to a general loss of confidence, so that up-to-date market prices for those assets are unavailable. It may become exceptionally difficult for the central bank to determine whether a bank seeking emergency short-term funding faces a temporary liquidity problem only, or is fundamentally insolvent. At the height of a crisis, and faced with the prospect that banks might collapse if short-term funding is withheld, central banks may err on the side of generosity in valuing assets. Before the crisis breaks, bank executives who anticipate that the lender-of-last-resort facility will be available if required may be inclined to take excessive risks in their lending.

In an effort to prevent bank runs, many countries have introduced deposit insurance schemes, guaranteed by governments and operated by government agencies. Deposit insurance provides a guarantee that bank depositors will always recover their deposits, even if the bank fails. Usually there is a maximum amount per depositor covered by the scheme. In many countries deposit insurance is funded by fees collected from banks, based on either size or risk or a combination of both. Crucially, however, the government guarantee ensures that the deposit insurance fund will always pay out when called upon to do so. If depositors believe they can always recover their funds, there should be no cause for them to trigger a bank run.

In the US deposit insurance for bank accounts is overseen by the FDIC. Before the global financial crisis, the deposit insurance limit was $100,000. This limit was increased to $250,000 at the height of the crisis in 2008. Before the crisis, all EU member states were required to operate a deposit guarantee scheme for at least 90 per cent of the deposited amount to a maximum of at least €20,000 per person. Deposit insurance coverage in all EU member states was increased to €100,000 by the end of 2010. In the UK the Financial Services Compensation Scheme protects bank deposits, along with insurance policies and personal investments. Since 2010 the scheme has the same coverage limits as those of other EU countries.

Like most forms of insurance, deposit insurance is subject to a moral hazard problem, if it encourages bankers or depositors to behave recklessly, or less carefully than they would otherwise. Bankers may be tempted adopt riskier lending practices in pursuit of higher returns, if they believe the risk of a run on the bank is mitigated by deposit insurance. Likewise depositors may be tempted to place their funds with banks that are able to offer higher returns as a result of their risky lending, if they know these deposits are guaranteed.

Another moral hazard dilemma, exposed ruthlessly by the global financial crisis, was a tendency for the scope of government guarantees and bailouts to extend far beyond the commitments entered into under deposit insurance. The too-big-to-fail (TBTF) problem in banking refers to the belief of creditors and executives of very large banks at the core of the financial system that they will always be bailed out by the government if the need arises, because the consequences of the failure of a very large bank for financial stability would be too damaging for the government to accept.

Such expectations of government intervention distort investors' incentives to price adequately the risks of banks they consider TBTF. Accordingly, TBTF banks can access funding at lower rates than their smaller counterparts. This distorts competition, and provides opportunities for large banks to grow even larger. Aware of the existence of a TBTF safety net, the executives of smaller institutions have an incentive to grow to a size consistent with TBTF status. By extending risky loans, or investing in risky assets in search of high returns, banks enjoy handsome profits if these loans and investments succeed, while the government, and ultimately the taxpayer, picks up the tab in the event of failure.

Concerns over TBTF must be set against the efficiency or average cost savings that may accrue to the largest banks. Empirical evidence reported in studies of cost structure in banking suggests that larger banks are able to supply banking services at a lower average cost per account or per customer than small banks. However, the very largest banks may have grown far beyond the maximum size at which average cost savings are achievable. In any event, measurement of the average cost savings achieved by the largest banks may be clouded by TBTF. If investors and depositors are convinced they will never incur losses because they anticipate a publicly funded bailout whenever one is required, TBTF banks will be able to raise funds (from investors and depositors) more cheaply than other banks. Therefore the average cost savings of the largest banks may derive, either wholly or partly, from the implicit public subsidy associated with TBTF status.

Sometimes banks (small or large) do fail, and when this happens the authorities require procedures for achieving an orderly resolution. The government may become closely involved in brokering a deal resulting in the acquisition of the distressed institution, taking partial or complete ownership itself through recapitalization using public funds, or resolution in cases of outright failure. Resolution procedures include interventions that can result in the closure of a distressed bank, or the creation of an asset-management company to administer the failing bank's remaining assets. Normal bankruptcy procedures are rarely used, owing to concerns over the wider financial and economic instability that might follow. Instead, special insolvency regimes have been tailored specifically for banks and financial institutions. These differ from country to country, and many of them have been revised since the global financial crisis.

Capital adequacy regulation

Capital or equity, the difference between total assets and total liabilities, is a key indicator of the solvency of a bank. It provides a buffer against losses arising from loans not being repaid or investments declining in value. If balance-sheet assets have to be written down in value, these losses are absorbed through a reduction in the bank's capital. A bank whose capital has been wiped out completely is no longer solvent. As soon as the bank's creditors (depositors or other parties who have lent funds to the bank, for example by purchasing bonds issued by the bank) realize that the total value of the bank's liabilities exceeds the total value of its assets, they will demand repayment and the bank, unable to meet these demands, will collapse. Regulation imposes minimum capital adequacy requirements on banks to minimize the risk of failure.

As seen in Chapter 2, the amount of capital a bank holds affects the returns accruing to the bank's shareholders, and also the risk associated with their investment. Other things being equal, the more capital a bank holds, the smaller is the return received by shareholders, but the smaller too is the risk that the shareholders will see the value of their capital wiped out by unforeseen losses.

Capital regulation for banks was introduced in 1988 by the Basel Committee on Banking Supervision at the Bank for International Settlements (BIS). Headquartered in Basel, Switzerland, BIS promotes international cooperation in the pursuit of monetary and financial stability, and acts as a banker to central banks. The central banks of sixty mainly large or developed countries are the members and owners of BIS. The Basel I Accord set down agreed capital standards developed by supervisors and central banks. Basel I required internationally active banks to maintain a capital ratio of at least 8 per cent: in other words, to hold capital equivalent to at least 8 per cent of risk-weighted assets. The risk weightings are as follows: 0 per cent (cash, reserves, government securities); 20 per cent (claims on banks in OECD countries); 50 per cent (municipal bonds, residential mortgages), and 100 per cent (loans to consumers and corporations). The capital ratio is (Tier 1 capital + Tier 2 capital)/Risk-weighted assets, where Tier 1 capital is shareholder capital plus retained earnings or disclosed reserves, and Tier 2 capital is undisclosed reserves, general loss reserves, and subordinated debt. Table 5 illustrates the calculation of the capital ratio.

Basel I was simple to understand, transparent, and provided incentives for banks to hold highly liquid, low-risk assets. Almost all countries with developed banking systems transposed Basel I into national law. However, Basel I focused solely on the credit risk associated with lending, and ignored other sources of risk. Subsequently amendments required banks to hold capital against market risk. Banks were encouraged to use internal risk-assessment models to measure their exposure to market risk, dependent on the composition of their assets portfolios.

Basel II, launched in 2006, established a three-pillar framework comprising minimum capital requirements (Pillar 1); supervisory review (Pillar 2); and market discipline (Pillar 3). For Pillar 1, the definition of capital remained unchanged, but the risk-weightings reflected credit, market, and operational risk. The calculations relied heavily on the banks' own internal risk measurement models, and on ratings provided by credit-rating agencies such as Standard & Poor's, Moody's, and Fitch IBCA. Pillar 2 required national supervisors to review the capital adequacy provisions of

Table 5 Calculating risk-based capital under Basel I

Assets	$bn	Liabilities	$bn
Cash	6	Deposits	540
Government bonds	80	Subordinated debt	15
Interbank loans	60	Loan-loss reserves	9
Mortgages	150		
Corporate loans	309	**Total liabilities**	564
		Total capital/equity (includes retained earnings)	41
Total assets	605	**Total liabilities and capital**	605

Tier 1 capital = Equity (including retained earnings) = 41
Tier 2 Capital = Loan-loss reserves + Subordinated debt = 9 + 15 = 24
Total Capital = Tier 1 Capital + Tier 2 Capital = 41 + 24 = 65
Total assets = 605
Capital-to-assets ratio = 65/605 = 10.74%
Basel I risk-weighted assets (asset category × risk-weight)
$= (6 \times 0) + (80 \times 0) + (60 \times 0.2) + (150 \times 0.5) + (309 \times 1)$
$= 12 + 75 + 309 = 396$
Basel I capital ratio = 65 /396 = 16.41%

each bank. Supervisors have the discretion to require banks to hold capital above the minimum regulatory requirements. Pillar 3 requires banks to disclose information regarding risk exposures, capital adequacy, and other material details. It was intended that greater reliance should be placed on market discipline as a constraint on risk-taking behaviour. Forward-looking market-based information embodied in banks' share and bond prices and ratings can inform supervision, and provide early warning of the need for supervisory intervention.

Basel II was never fully implemented, owing to the onset of the global financial crisis, which exposed weaknesses in capital regulation. Risk-based capital ratios were supposedly superior measures of capital adequacy; but their usefulness was dependent on the accurate measurement of risk. The financial crisis damaged the credibility of the banks' internal models for risk measurement, damaged the reputations of the credit-rating agencies, and raised doubts about the effectiveness of market discipline as a constraint on risk-taking. Furthermore, Basel II may have amplified the business cycle because it is pro-cyclical. During buoyant economic conditions, risk is perceived to be low and lending tends to increase. Banks extend what ultimately turn out to be poor-quality loans, without accumulating sufficient capital. During a recession, conversely, loan delinquencies deplete capital, while a mood of pessimism suggests capital should be increased. Banks hold insufficient capital to absorb losses, and scramble to improve their capital ratios by reducing lending, leading to credit rationing. Changes to international capital regulation since the global financial crisis are described in Chapter 8.

Other forms of regulation

In many countries consumers have access to a broad range of savings products, and borrow from a choice of lenders. However, there is abundant evidence that many consumers lack the information, skills, and knowledge to make informed choices. Several factors create a need for consumer protection regulation of banking and other financial services. Some financial products are purchased infrequently, and consumers may have limited opportunity to learn from their mistakes. Terms and conditions of financial products can be opaque, requiring specialized knowledge to judge the quality of the product before, during, and after consumption. Many financial products require consumers to commit to long-term contracts with uncertain outcomes that may only become apparent at maturity. A tendency for consumers to make poor financial decisions has been blamed on low financial literacy, including a failure to understand basic concepts such as compound interest. Lack of financial literacy makes consumers vulnerable to scams perpetrated by unscrupulous financial-services providers. In the US the Consumer Financial Protection Bureau (CFPB) was formed under the Dodd–Frank Act in 2010 to oversee consumer protection, and enforce consumer financial regulations. The Directorate General for Health and Consumers is responsible for consumer protection within the EU. In the UK since April 2014, the FCA has been responsible for consumer protection in financial services. The FCA also assumed responsibility for aspects of consumer credit, previously the responsibility for the Office of Fair Trading.

For most industries, competition policy is guided by the principle that competition between suppliers is beneficial for consumers. For banking, however, the comparison between an open market with intense competition, and one that is highly regulated with restrictions imposed upon competition, is by no means clear-cut. One view, known as the competition-fragility view, is that restrictions imposed upon competition between banks enhance financial stability. In the absence of competitive pressure, incumbent banks can earn monopoly profits and accumulate capital in the form of retained profits. This strengthens their capacity to absorb unanticipated losses, and discourages excessive risk-taking that carries the potential to destroy shareholder value. To the contrary, the competition-stability view suggests that restrictions on competition between banks give rise to financial instability. If incumbent banks exercise monopoly power, they tend to set higher interest rates for borrowers. Higher rates encourage borrowers to accept more risk in their investments or other activities in search of returns sufficient to service the original loan, or give borrowers stronger incentives to default. All of this tends to make the financial system less stable.

In the US the Federal Trade Commission (FTC) and the Department of Justice (DOJ) are involved in administering anti-trust (competition) law. The cornerstones of EU competition policy are Articles 101 and 102 of the Treaty of Lisbon of 2009. Article 101 deals with restrictive practices, while Article 102 regulates possible abuses of monopoly power. In accordance with the principle of subsidiarity, the scope of Articles 101 and 102 is confined to firms based in EU member states that trade in other EU states. In the UK, until 2012 competition policy was the responsibility of the Office of Fair Trading (OFT) and the Competition Commission. At the height of the financial crisis large bank mergers, such as HBOS and Lloyds TSB, were waved through, on the grounds that preventing collapse was more important than fostering competition. In March 2012 the UK government announced the creation of a new Competition and Markets Authority (CMA), consolidating the Competition Commission and the OFT into a single entity.

Chapter 6
Origins of the global financial crisis

The global financial crisis of 2007–9 is widely considered to have been the most severe crisis since the Great Depression of the 1930s. In the interim, localized banking or financial crises occurred many different countries. During the two decades prior to the global financial crisis, several of these crises contained warnings of the upheaval that was to come.

The Swedish banking crisis

During the 1980s, the Swedish government pursued a policy of low interest rates. This encouraged excessive borrowing and an increase in residential property prices. When interest rates increased in 1990 borrowers found it increasingly difficult to service debts, loan defaults increased, and property prices fell. Write-offs of delinquent loans eroded the capital of Swedish banks, triggering a banking crisis that began in autumn 1991. The Swedish government nationalized the ailing Nordbanken, and set up a 'bad bank' to administer Nordbanken's non-performing assets. The crisis peaked in September 1992, when Gota Bank became insolvent.

A few weeks later the Swedish government announced a state guarantee of all bank deposits and creditors of 114 Swedish banks. State funds were made available for the recapitalization of ailing banks, but the banks were required to clean up their balance sheets by writing off bad assets before applying for state assistance. The banks' shareholders were required to absorb the losses incurred under their watch, prior to the crisis. This decisive action allowed the government to liquidate delinquent assets and minimize the costs to the taxpayer. The initial cost of the rescue was approximately 4 per cent of Swedish GDP. Subsequent sales of assets acquired by the government through nationalization or recapitalization reduced the estimated cost to between 0 per cent and 2 per cent of GDP. At the height of the global financial crisis of 2007–9, the Swedish government's handling of the 1991–3 banking crisis was cited by some commentators as a role model.

The US Savings and Loan crisis

Until the mid-1980s Savings and Loan (S&L) associations (thrifts) were prominent lenders in the US mortgage market. Constituted similarly to UK building societies, S&Ls accepted deposits and granted mortgages and personal loans to individual members. S&Ls held a high proportion of their assets in mortgage loans. When interest rates increased sharply as a consequence of the recession of the late 1970s and early 1980s, the S&Ls were exposed to large losses, owing to mismatch between their assets and liabilities. Their funding costs, the rates paid to depositors, increased, while the revenues earned from a high proportion of fixed interest rate mortgages on their books remained static. Many S&Ls became technically insolvent, but rather than enforce immediate closure the regulatory authorities exercised forbearance, allowing them to remain in business in the hope that recovery could be achieved. Meanwhile financial deregulation reduced the amount of capital S&Ls were required to hold, and extended the range of loans they could offer. By increasing rates the S&Ls were able to attract new depositors. This funding was used to extend riskier loans in areas such as commercial property. There were many cases of creative accounting to mask losses or insolvency, and some cases of outright fraud.

Between 1986 and 1995 more than 1,000 S&Ls, around one-third of the total, were subject to closure or other forms of resolution. The US government set up the Resolution Trust Corporation in 1989 to resolve the assets of failed S&Ls, and transferred responsibility for deposit insurance from the Federal Savings and Loan Insurance Corporation (FSLIC), which had become insolvent, to the FDIC. The heavy costs prompted Congress to pass the FDIC Improvement Act of 1991 (FDICIA), requiring the FDIC to resolve failed banks in a manner that minimized the cost to taxpayers. Only insured depositors and creditors would be fully protected in the event of failure. However, the legislation allowed for exceptional circumstances in which all depositors and creditors could be protected, if failure to protect would create financial instability.

The Japanese banking crisis

Following a period of financial deregulation, increased competition in the banking and financial sectors, and a property market boom which ended in 1990–1, Japan entered a banking crisis. The collapse in property prices plunged a number of Jusen, privately-owned non-bank financial companies that specialized in mortgage lending, into severe financial difficulties. The balance sheets of Japanese banks were hit by their exposures to the Jusen. The initial response of the Japanese Ministry of Finance has been characterized as one of 'regulatory forbearance': the banks were allowed considerable leeway in determining the extent to which they wrote down bad loans, and were not encouraged to recapitalize by issuing new capital (equity). Following a weak economic recovery during the mid-1990s, Japan experienced a further macroeconomic downturn at the onset of the Asian crisis in 1997, which produced a major, systemic banking and financial crisis. The failure of Sanyo Securities in November 1997 triggered a slowdown in interbank lending and an increase in interbank rates. In quick succession Hokkaido Takushoku Bank, Yamaichi Securities, and Tokuyo City Bank all collapsed. Between 1998 and

2000 several measures were introduced to stabilize the financial system: temporary government control or closure of insolvent institutions; publicly-funded capital injections; strengthening deposit-insurance guarantees; the creation of asset-management companies to acquire delinquent loans; and changes in loan-loss provisioning rules.

The government response to the crisis was criticized as slow and uncoordinated. Two banks that were recapitalized in 1998 failed subsequently, leading to full nationalization. This episode highlighted the need to clean balance sheets by writing off delinquent loans, making existing shareholders bear the losses, before injecting new capital. Public confidence in the banks remained low. The banks found it difficult to recapitalize in the face of low profitability and a general reluctance on the part of investors to inject new capital. The ability of banks to extend finance to the corporate sector was curtailed for an extended period, with small and medium-sized enterprises (SMEs) especially hard-hit. For two 'lost decades', the Japanese economy experienced a protracted deflationary spiral.

The Asian financial crisis

After opening up their goods and services markets to outside competition, several South East Asian economies experienced annual growth rates averaging around 8 per cent over the period 1987–97. Per capita income increased dramatically. Over the same period South East Asian countries collectively doubled their share of world exports to approximately 20 per cent. These countries were also major consumers of foreign goods, making their economies attractive to foreign investors and banks. Bank lending on favourable terms to non-financial companies (especially large industrial conglomerates with relatively poor economic performance) increased dramatically. Inadequate regulation and supervision led to banks becoming over exposed in sectors such as electronics, property, and tourism.

As market conditions deteriorated and bank losses increased the foreign exchange markets witnessed a series of speculative attacks, from July 1997 onwards, on the currencies of Thailand (baht), Philippines (peso), Indonesia (rupiah), Malaysia (ringgit), and South Korea (won). Large declines in currency values created difficulties for companies in these countries that had taken bank loans denominated in foreign currencies. Central banks raised interest rates in an attempt to stem the flight of capital, but often ineffectively. Fearful of the panic spreading beyond South East Asia, the International Monetary Fund (IMF) extended bailout loans to countries, conditional on reforms to their financial systems and economies. Stability in South East Asian financial markets was eventually restored, but only after deep recessions, and political upheaval in Indonesia and Thailand.

The Asian financial crisis is instructive for several reasons: first, as a case study in contagion, with numerous countries having been affected within a very short period; second, for the severity of the recessions in the countries affected, as well as the rapid speed at which they recovered subsequently; and third, for the longer-term policy responses of several affected countries that restructured their economies so as to run large current account surpluses, and accumulate foreign currency reserves capable of withstanding possible future speculative attacks. This latter policy resulted in an ever-increasing supply of funding for the sovereign debt of the US and other western countries during the 2000s, which may have fuelled the stock-market and housing bubbles in western economies that preceded the global financial crisis.

Causes of the 2007–9 global financial crisis

For many years prior to the global financial crisis, the world economy had been subject to large and persistent macroeconomic imbalances. Several countries in South and East Asia, and in the Gulf region, ran large surpluses on the current accounts of their balance of payments, so that the value of their exports exceeded the value of imports. These countries channelled a high proportion of the revenues earned from exports into savings, rather than current consumption. By contrast, western countries including the US (the world's largest economy) and western European nations, ran large current account deficits, so that the value of their imports exceeded the value of exports. Current account deficits were typically financed by borrowing. In other words, western countries spent more than they earned, and borrowed the difference.

Economists disagree over the apportionment of blame for the crisis between global macroeconomic imbalances, and policy mistakes committed by the Federal Reserve and the central banks of other deficit countries. Defenders of the Federal Reserve argue that the cheap and plentiful credit available for borrowing by households, companies, and governments in the deficit countries originated mainly from surplus country savings. Critics argue that excessively lax monetary policy implemented by the Federal Reserve itself was primarily responsible for the explosion of borrowing. The latter was also fuelled by the global trend towards the deregulation of financial markets, which had been underway for two decades or more prior to the crisis. Throughout the early and mid-2000s the deficit countries were able to maintain low interest rates and high borrowing, without stoking inflation. The increasing debt, however, threatened to cause widespread problems of insolvency in the event of an interest rate hike or an interruption to the supply of cheap credit. This threat duly materialized when a large portion of the lending in deficit countries, which had been repackaged into securities held by deficit- and surplus-country investors alike, turned out to be toxic.

Mortgage lending to all categories of borrower in the US grew strongly during the early and mid-2000s. One particular borrower category, 'subprime' borrowers whose credit history does not qualify them for a conventional mortgage, has achieved notoriety. During the years before the global financial crisis, the standards applied by both bank and non-bank lenders in determining whether to grant mortgages were eroded dramatically, resulting in an explosion of lending in general, and in particular to high-risk borrowers. Between 2001 and 2003 the share of subprime loans in total US mortgage originations was below 10 per cent. This figure increased to around 20 per cent between 2004 and 2006, when the house price bubble reached its peak. Much subprime lending took the form of adjustable rate mortgages (ARMs), with an initial 'teaser' fixed rate of interest that would reset to a higher, flexible rate after two years. Commonly the principal (amount borrowed) was so high that the subprime borrower's financial resources were stretched to the limit in servicing the loan at the teaser rate; in such cases the borrower had no chance of keeping up the repayments when the higher rate kicked in after two years. Some mortgages allowed even riskier options from the lender's perspective. Option ARMs and negative amortization ARMs offered borrowers monthly choices such as payment of interest only, in which case the repayment of principal was deferred, or no monthly payment, in which case the interest foregone by the lender was added to the loan outstanding.

At the time, the practice of lending to borrowers who carried a high risk of never being able to repay may have seemed justified by ever-rising house prices. Provided house price inflation continued, borrowers would accumulate sufficient equity in their houses to refinance their mortgages after two years, repaying the old ARM to avoid the higher rate of interest, and taking out a new ARM for the same or an even larger principal. By increasing the size of the loan, the borrower could extract the gain in equity in the form of a lump sum. If house prices dropped, however, the refinancing option would not be available, and the mortgage would be likely to default when the teaser rate expired. In the US, in some cases a homeowner who is unable to service a mortgage can simply vacate the house and return the keys to the mortgage lender. The house is repossessed and the lender assumes responsibility for recovering the loan by selling the house.

Between 1997 and 2006 the price of the average US house increased by 124 per cent. The house price bubble peaked at the start of 2006, and prices had fallen by about 30 per cent by 2009. From 2006 mortgage delinquencies soared, just as a glut of newly built and repossessed houses came onto the market. Lenders often recovered only a fraction of the original loan values by selling repossessed houses in a falling market. Housing market bubbles also occurred in a number of other countries: most notably Spain and Ireland, as well as the UK and several other European countries.

Serious delinquencies (mortgages with payments more than ninety days overdue or in foreclosure) may have accounted for more than 40 per cent of all subprime ARMs in the US by the end of 2009. Large fees and commissions provided the incentives for individuals to overlook or actively hasten the erosion of lending standards at all stages of the mortgage supply chain: the mortgage brokers that arranged the loans for the borrowers; the retail banks that lent the money; the large investment banks that dealt with the mechanics of securitization when the mortgages were repackaged and sold to investors; and the credit-rating agencies that testified to the safety of complex and inadequately understood asset-backed securities.

Securitization (see Chapter 3) enabled banks to convert illiquid mortgage (and other) loans into marketable securities by slicing streams of anticipated income streams into low-, medium-, and high-risk tranches, thereby releasing capital to support other investments. Securitization became popular, in part, because by moving a pool of loans (assets) into a Structured Investment Vehicle (SIV) that was not subject to regulation, banks were able to avoid the need to hold capital against these securitized assets. In principle the trade in securitized assets and credit derivatives should improve the efficiency and stability of the financial system, by transferring risk to those investors most willing or equipped to bear risk. In practice, securitization was a contributory factor to the financial crisis, by heightening problems of adverse selection and moral hazard. Securitization weakened the incentive for originating lenders to screen borrowers prior to lending and monitor their performance subsequently. Originating lenders failed to complete basic tasks fundamental to their role as financial intermediaries, because they anticipated that the loans would be repackaged and passed on to other investors who would bear the credit risk.

Securitization increased opacity and complexity throughout the financial system, since it became unclear where the losses arising from potential future loan defaults would accrue. It became difficult or impossible for investors to assess the risks being run by financial institutions independently of the scores produced by the credit-rating agencies, which turned out to be flawed. It later transpired that much of the credit risk never actually left the balance sheets of the banks, since the banks and their SIVs were themselves among the most prolific traders of securitized assets. By distancing the borrower from the ultimate lender, securitization invited fraudulent practice on the part of some borrowers, who did not accurately disclose their financial circumstances, and some mortgage originators, who knowingly encouraged households to borrow far beyond their means.

It is widely accepted that the major credit-rating agencies (Moody's, Standard & Poor's, and Fitch IBCA) were inadvertently complicit in exacerbating the crisis. Credit-rating agencies offer judgements regarding the credit risk (quality) of bonds issued by large companies, financial institutions, and governments, summarized in an alphabetical scale of grades. The best-known scale is Standard & Poor's, in which the top grade is 'AAA', denoting very high-quality assets (with minimal credit risk), and the lowest is 'BB', denoting low-quality or 'junk' bonds (with a high probability of default). The credit-rating agencies were influential in determining the returns banks could earn by securitizing pools of mortgages and selling the resulting mortgage-backed securities

(MBS) to third-party investors. The proceeds from such sales were directly related to the agencies' ratings of the tranches of securitized assets: banks (or SIVs set up by banks) would pay the lowest interest on the most highly rated tranches. Furthermore, regulations stipulated that banks themselves could only buy tranches that were highly rated.

With the benefit of hindsight, it is clear that the credit-rating agencies were subject to conflicts of interest when preparing ratings for MBS and other securities commissioned and paid for by the issuing banks themselves, but presented to investors as the agencies' independent assessment of risk. The practice of 'ratings shopping' involved the issuers of securities sounding out the agencies for their initial feedback, and hiring the agency that quoted the most favourable rating. Alternatively, issuers could ask the agencies for advice on the adjustments that would be required to secure a higher rating, or enter into negotiations with the agencies. Higher agency fees for rating securitized assets than conventional bonds gave further encouragement for the production of favourable ratings.

Even if the conflicts of interest are set aside, the methods used by the agencies to produce their ratings were deeply flawed. Statistical models attached insufficient weight to events that would impact in a similar manner across the entire financial system, such as a nationwide decline in house prices as opposed to a localized decline. In other words the agencies underestimated systemic risk, as did many investors and regulators.

Until the late 1990s, banks valued their assets at historical cost, rather than current market value. Following the misreporting scandals of the early 2000s that precipitated the collapse of several major US corporations, such as Enron and WorldCom, the professional accountancy bodies and regulators introduced mark-to-market accounting rules, requiring balance-sheet valuations of assets, especially investments in securities, to reflect current market values (fair value). If market prices were unavailable for securities that were thinly traded, then valuations could be based on those of similar securities for which prices were available. Alternatively, banks could employ their own statistical models to determine fair value. During the financial crisis these accounting rules contributed to a squeeze on banks' balance sheets. As the markets for many securities seized up, by the rules banks were obliged to report significantly lower valuations of their investment portfolios. Deteriorating bank balance sheets increased investors' perceptions of credit risk, contributing to a scarcity of short-term interbank funding, and placing banks that were reliant on the interbank markets under severe pressure.

Corporate governance refers to the systems by which companies are directed and controlled. Agency theory, which describes the conflicts of interest that can arise between a company's shareholders acting as principal, and its management acting as agent, is central to any discussion of corporate governance. A key question is whether the maximization of shareholder value is the only legitimate objective of a privately-owned enterprise, or whether the company should accept a wider range of responsibilities towards a broader constituency of stakeholders including employees, customers, taxpayers, and society in general. Executives' personal and professional attitudes play a key role in determining the degree of alignment of executive interests with shareholder interests, and the extent to which executives pursue the maximization of shareholder value. Much of the evidence suggests that both the level and composition of executive compensation affect the risk of financial institutions. Share options, which give executives the option to purchase shares in the company after the elapse of a defined time period at a pre-determined price, are seen as particularly culpable in increasing financial instability. Share options encourage executives to undertake riskier investments that offer the potential to drive up the company's share price in the short term, at the cost of piling up risk that can eventually explode.

It is widely recognized that in the run-up to the global financial crisis, the structure of the compensation schemes of the banks' top executives and traders created perverse incentives for excessive risk-taking. If a bank's risky investments turn out to be successful, the bank's top executives take the credit for the profits yielded by the investments, and are rewarded with generous bonus payments. If the investments are unsuccessful, the top executives still draw their salaries, or in a worst-case scenario might be encouraged to vacate their posts voluntarily by an attractive 'golden parachute' payment offer. Likewise the traders who execute the risky investments are rewarded with huge bonuses if the investments succeed, while the downside risk is nothing worse than a change of job if the investments fail.

By contrast, the bank's shareholders may share in the upside gains if the investments succeed and some of the profits are either paid out in dividends or retained, bolstering the value of the bank's capital. But shareholders also bear substantial downside risk, in the sense that any trading losses will deplete the bank's capital. Bondholders also bear downside risk, without any prospect of sharing in the upside gains. The bondholders' returns are fixed provided the bank remains solvent; but if the bank's capital is wiped out by trading losses, bondholders may be unable to recover the nominal value of their holdings upon redemption. All of this suggests that in the run-up to the crisis, top executives and traders developed a much stronger appetite for high-risk investment or trading strategies than the shareholders and bondholders whose money was used to finance these activities.

The diversification of credit risk through securitization did not eliminate liquidity risk, arising from maturity mismatch between the short time-horizons of banks' liabilities, and the long time-horizons of their assets. SIVs funded a significant portion of their investments by selling short-term or medium-term asset-backed securities (backed by the assets held by the SIV) on the money markets. SIVs were therefore subject to liquidity risk, owing to the mismatch between the very short-term maturity profile of their liabilities on the one hand, and their longer-term assets on the other. The growth of repo financing, involving the very short-term (overnight) sale and repurchase of collateralized assets on the balance sheets of investment banks (see Chapter 3) further increased the exposure of the system to liquidity risk. At any time, uncertainty over a financial institution's health might cause investors to cease rolling over the short-term debt that funds the long-term investments. This liquidity risk often reverted directly back to the parent bank, which might have granted either a contractual credit line providing its SIV with guaranteed access to funding, or a reputational credit line providing non-contractual access, which was nonetheless commonly granted in practice, motivated by concerns that the SIV's failure would destroy the parent bank's reputation.

It is inevitable that the regulatory authorities, tasked with ensuring the safety and stability of the financial system, should be subject to intense critical scrutiny in the event of a monumental systemic failure on the scale of the global financial crisis. Clearly the regulators failed to recognize the scale and significance of the explosion in US subprime mortgage lending prior to 2007. In the area of housing, the dominant free-market ideology of the day, to which chief regulators such as Alan Greenspan, Chair of the Federal Reserve from 1988 to 2006, enthusiastically subscribed, may have combined with longstanding political pressures in favour of promoting home ownership among low-income families in shaping the policies of the government-sponsored enterprises (GSEs) Fannie Mae and Freddie Mac. Originally created to increase the flow of funds into housing and create a liquid secondary market for trade in existing mortgages and mortgage-backed securities (MBS), the GSEs were shareholder-owned, but their debt was guaranteed by the US Treasury. This government guarantee had given the GSEs a crucial competitive edge, enabling them to capture a large share of the US mortgage market, and allowing them to operate with exceptionally highly leveraged balance sheets. Official enthusiasm for widening home ownership also provided cover for the regulators' predisposition to turn a blind eye to the general proliferation of unsafe lending standards. Much of the growth in subprime lending in the US during the 2000s was fuelled by mortgages issued not by the banks themselves, but by mortgage brokers operating outside the regulated banking system. Such brokers originated the loans, and then sold them on within a few days or weeks for securitization.

A tolerance for the avoidance by banks of regulatory constraints may be included on the charge-sheet against the regulators. The practice whereby banks transferred securitized assets to SIVs, wholly-owned subsidiaries whose assets and liabilities did not appear on the parent bank's balance sheet, allowed the total capital held throughout the entire (regulated and unregulated) banking system against the underlying assets to be reduced. For example, while the senior tranches of MBS with the highest credit ratings and low capital requirements were often retained by regulated banks, the junior tranches were commonly channelled via the SIV into the unregulated shadow banking system, escaping the higher regulatory capital requirements their risk profile would otherwise have demanded.

Credit derivatives were another key financial innovation of the years preceding the crisis which largely escaped regulatory oversight. Securities such as credit default swaps (CDS) were tailor-made to meet the requirements of the parties entering into the contract, and traded by means of negotiation between the buyer and seller in unregulated over-the-counter (OTC) markets. This is in contrast to many other securities, such as government bonds, company shares, and some derivatives, which are written with standardized terms and conditions, and traded through organized exchanges that act as central clearing-houses for processing purchase and sale transactions. The ability to negotiate bilateral contracts with complex terms and conditions enabled participants in OTC credit derivatives markets to fine-tune the hedging of their risk exposures (and may also have protected high fees for the engineering of complex financial products that would have been eroded through competition had there been more standardization). However, the complexity and lack of standardization created a lack of transparency throughout the financial system, because no-one knew precisely the magnitude of the total risk exposures or where they were concentrated.

In view of the insurance-like nature of CDS, the lack of regulation contrasts starkly with the situation for traditional forms of insurance, which are heavily regulated. Regulation enables a consumer who takes out life insurance with a large company such as American International Group (AIG) to feel confident that AIG will still be around to pay out in the event of the policyholder's death. By contrast, the banks that purchased CDS from AIG, in some cases to protect themselves from losses that would be incurred in the event of the failure of other banks, had no regulatory protection whatsoever. Given the opacity of the linkages between financial institutions, it is easy to see how the failure of one large institution could rapidly cause panic over the solvency of many others.

Chapter 7
The global financial crisis and the Eurozone sovereign debt crisis

According to estimates, seven years after the peak of the global financial crisis in 2008, the combined GDP of OECD member countries in 2015 was around 10 per cent lower than it would have been if the pre-crisis trend in GDP had been maintained. This might be an over estimate of the effect of the crisis, however, since the pre-crisis trend reflects several boom years when economies were growing rapidly and perhaps unsustainably. If the comparison is made with potential GDP, a measure of the long-term trend in GDP that is sustainable, the combined GDP of OECD member countries was 6 per cent or 7 per cent lower than it would have been if the pre-crisis trend had been maintained. Whatever the precise figure, few economists would dispute that the recession which followed the crisis was the deepest since the Great Depression of the 1930s.

The United States

Early indications of the imminent financial crisis in the US were visible during the first half of 2007, as the rate of subprime mortgage delinquencies soared, resulting in sharp reductions in the prices of mortgage-backed securities (MBS), and increases in the cost of insuring these securities against default. Ratings downgrades were announced by several credit-rating agencies in June and July 2007. The investment bank Bear Stearns liquidated two hedge funds with large MBS portfolios, and several large mortgage lenders filed for bankruptcy protection. Overnight interbank lending rates increased sharply on 9 August 2007, after BNP Paribas announced that it was halting redemptions on three of its investment funds. Although the Federal Reserve and the European Central Bank (ECB) responded by injecting $24bn and €95bn, respectively, into the interbank markets, volumes of interbank lending fell sharply; and liquidity in the market for short-term asset-backed securities also began to dry up.

The crisis escalated during the spring of 2008 with the collapse of Bear Stearns, the smallest of the 'big five' US investment banks. In response to rumours circulating in financial markets that Bear Stearns was experiencing liquidity difficulties, in March 2008 the Federal Reserve Bank of New York announced that it would provide a $25 billion emergency loan; subsequently this offer was rescinded. Two days later Bear Stearns entered into a merger agreement with JPMorgan Chase, which valued Bear Stearns at $2 per share, down from $172 per share as recently as January 2007. The new company was funded by loans of $29bn from the FRB New York, and $1bn from JPMorgan Chase. Subsequently JPMorgan Chase's offer was raised to $10 per share, in an attempted compromise with disgruntled Bear Stearns shareholders. The latter eventually approved the sale in May.

The FDIC assumed responsibility for the management of the ailing Savings and Loan (S&L) association IndyMac in July 2008. Origination and securitization of Alt-A mortgages (a category considered riskier than prime but less risky than subprime) had been a major element in IndyMac's aggressive growth strategy during the years prior to its collapse. Unable to find a private-sector purchaser, the FDIC took control of the remainder of IndyMac's mortgages portfolio, and proceeded to implement a series of measures designed to reduce the number of defaults, including interest rate reductions, extensions of maturities, and reductions of principal outstanding.

On 7 September 2008 it was announced that the two government-sponsored enterprises (GSEs), Fannie Mae and Freddie Mac, would be placed under the control of their regulator, the Federal Housing Finance Authority. Traditionally restricted to dealing in high-quality mortgages only, prior to the crisis the two GSEs had accumulated significant portfolios of subprime MBS, spurred on by their public mission to support affordable housing. Delinquent mortgage write-offs during 2006 and 2007 were sufficient to deplete the GSEs' modest capital base, rendering them insolvent. By 2012 the two GSEs are estimated to have absorbed around $190bn of public bailout funding, returning $46bn in dividends.

Following the collapse of Bear, the attentions of speculators turned rapidly to Lehman Brothers, the fourth-largest US investment bank. Lehman's business model replicated many of the features that had undermined its smaller rival, including high leverage, over-reliance on short-term borrowing, and heavy exposures in MBS. Additionally, Lehman had accumulated large real-estate investments in commercial property. As its solvency deteriorated during summer 2008, Lehman made overtures to several potential merger partners or acquirers in the hope of securing a substantial capital injection. Over the weekend of 12–14 September, negotiations with Barclays stalled over the US Treasury's refusal to commit any public funding to support the takeover. Having attracted stinging public criticism for the publicly-funded rescue of Bear, and after having given open-ended commitments to the GSEs only one week previously, the Treasury took the fateful decision to sacrifice Lehman. On 15 September Lehman filed for Chapter 11 bankruptcy protection (Figure 12).

Why did the Treasury refuse to bail out Lehman after having previously rescued Bear Stearns (and the GSEs)? Several explanations have been suggested: first, after witnessing Bear's failure the markets had ample time to prepare for and adjust to the anticipated collapse of Lehman; second, although Lehman

12. Lehman Brothers' failure.

was twice the size of Bear, Bear may have been more interconnected with other financial institutions than Lehman; and third, the decision was simply a matter of timing, with the Treasury feeling it needed to draw a 'line in the sand' at some stage on bailouts. According to Alan Blinder, the absence of any private-sector guarantor for a possible Federal Reserve loan was the crucial distinction drawn between Lehman and Bear (whose bailout loan was part-guaranteed by JPMorgan Chase). The lack of a private-sector suitor may have reflected the markets' judgement that while Bear's collapse was caused by a shortage of liquidity, Lehman was fundamentally insolvent.

Whatever the justification for the Treasury's refusal to bail out Lehman, this momentous decision triggered a spectacular sequence of events that brought the global financial system to the brink of catastrophe. On 14 September the third-largest investment bank, Merrill Lynch, was hastily acquired by Bank of America for $50bn, amid reports of a loss of confidence in the bank's ability to refinance its short-term debt.

On 16 September the Federal Reserve acquired an 80 per cent stake in the largest US insurer, American International Group (AIG), in return for a loan of $85bn, subsequently increased to $182bn. AIG had accumulated a massive portfolio of credit default swaps (CDS), providing insurance against defaults on subprime MBS and other structured products. AIG's exposure on tranches of securitized products with the highest AAA credit rating was estimated at $450bn. AIG had failed to hedge the risk by taking offsetting positions in other securities that would pay out in the event that AIG was required to pay out on its CDS portfolio. AIG had also neglected to set aside capital reserves commensurate with its CDS exposure. The bailout took place despite grave concerns over AIG's solvency as well as its liquidity.

On 16 September the Reserve Primary Fund, a large money market fund, announced that its net asset value per share had fallen below $1, primarily owing to losses on short-term debt issued by Lehman. In a successful attempt to stem a run on the money market funds, the Treasury announced it would deploy $50bn from the Exchange Stabilization Fund to guarantee all existing money market fund liabilities; and the Federal Reserve made loans available to purchasers of asset-backed commercial paper (ABCP) from money market funds.

On 21 September it was announced that the Federal Reserve had approved the applications of Goldman Sachs and Morgan Stanley, the two remaining survivors (and the two largest) of the five major US investment banks, to convert to bank holding company status, making them eligible to be bailed out using public funds if necessary. This move appears to have dampened market speculation that these two investment banks might follow a similar path towards meltdown as their ex-competitors Merrill Lynch, Lehman Brothers, and Bear Stearns.

On 25 September the banking operations of Washington Mutual (WaMu), the largest S&L with assets of $307bn, the sixth-largest

US bank and the third-largest mortgage lender, was sold to JPMorgan Chase for $1.9bn. The sale followed a run on deposits, triggered by depositor concerns over the quality of WaMu's mortgage portfolio. An important precedent was set when, in stark contrast to Bear and AIG, WaMu's bondholders and unsecured creditors were forced to absorb losses. This development appears to have triggered a loss of confidence in Wachovia, the fourth-largest US bank. On 29 September a deal was announced for the acquisition of Wachovia by Citigroup; subsequently this deal broke down and Wachovia was purchased by Wells Fargo in a $15.1bn deal which did not involve any government support.

The US government's immediate response to these events was the Troubled Asset Relief Program (TARP), under which $700bn was earmarked for the purchase by the Treasury of troubled MBS, or any other securities deemed to be necessary to promote financial market stability. After the first version of TARP was voted down by Congress on 29 September, triggering large falls in stock prices, an amended version was hurriedly passed into law on 3 October. Subsequently in November Treasury Secretary Hank Paulson announced the abandonment of the original plan to purchase troubled assets, in favour of a policy of acquiring new ownership stakes in ailing banks whose balance sheets required capital injections. The change of direction appears to have been influenced by recognition of the difficulties in establishing a fair price for assets such as MBS in markets that had largely seized up.

In October it was announced that $250bn of TARP funds would be used for capital injections, with half of this amount assigned to nine large banks: Citigroup, JPMorgan Chase, Wells Fargo, Bank of America, Merrill Lynch, Goldman Sachs, Morgan Stanley, Bank of New York Mellon, and State Street. This recapitalization program was widely criticized for applying public funds indiscriminately to banks that required recapitalization, and to others that did not. The intention was to avoid stigmatizing recipients.

In November the Federal Reserve and Treasury announced an additional $800bn package, comprising $600bn for the purchase of MBS issued by the GSEs Fannie Mae and Freddie Mac, and a $200bn lending facility for institutions willing to purchase designated asset-backed securities. The purchase of GSE securities marked the first phase of quantitative easing, QE1 (see also Chapter 8). Meanwhile the bank bailouts continued. Citigroup, at the time the largest US bank, was rescued by the Treasury, Federal Reserve, and FDIC in a package announced in November. The Treasury had disposed of its stake in Citigroup by the end of 2010. In a major extension of the scope of public bailout funding, in December the US Treasury announced a $17.4bn package of TARP funding for General Motors and Chrysler. In total, the motor industry bailout is estimated to have ultimately cost the taxpayer around $9bn.

During 2008 Bank of America had acquired the mortgage lender Countrywide Financial, which had been heavily implicated in the subprime crisis, and had agreed to acquire Merrill Lynch in a deal that had not been completed by the end of the year. In January 2009 a bailout of Bank of America was announced, under terms similar to the Citigroup rescue. The bailout appears to have been partly motivated by the regulators' desire to ensure that the purchase of Merrill Lynch did not collapse. Although there were some further publicly-funded capital injections into banks in early 2009, Bank of America was the last major US bank bailout of the 2007–9 crisis.

The United Kingdom and the Eurozone

Many European banks incurred losses on investments in MBS and other securities that were backed by loans that turned out to be delinquent as a consequence of the US subprime crisis. In Germany, IKB Deutsche Industriebank was an early victim of the crisis. Between 2002 and 2007 IKB accumulated a €12.7bn portfolio of asset-backed securities, held off-balance sheet by its SIV, Rhineland Funding. In August 2007 the state-owned Kreditanstalt für Wiederaufbau (KfW), a major shareholder in IKB, provided liquidity support and wrote off substantial losses on IKB's loans portfolio. Other German bailouts included Sachsen LB, a small state-owned regional bank with a large subprime exposure, acquired by the largest of the state-owned regional banks, LLBW (Landesbank Baden-Württemberg), in August 2007 with loan guarantees provided by the state government of Saxony; and WestLB, which secured €5bn of loan guarantees in January 2008 from the North Rhine-Westphalia state government and a consortium of local banks.

In September 2007 the retail bank Northern Rock was the first major UK casualty of the crisis. After Northern Rock announced that it had received emergency financial support from the Bank of England, £1bn was withdrawn from the bank's high-street branches over a few days. To stop the run the UK government announced a full guarantee of the bank's retail deposits. Subsequently Northern Rock was taken into public ownership.

During September 2008 Lloyds TSB announced that it was to acquire HBOS for £12bn, creating the Lloyds Banking Group, with a market share of around one-third in the UK savings and mortgage markets; and the UK government announced its acquisition of the mortgage-lending arm of Bradford & Bingley. The still-viable depositor base and branch network was sold to the Spanish Santander group.

In October the UK government announced the creation of a £50bn fund for the recapitalization of distressed banks. Capital injections were announced for RBS (£20bn), and Lloyds (£17bn), increasing the public ownership stakes in these banks to around 60 per cent and 40 per cent, respectively. In November an 'arms-length' company, UK Financial Investments Limited (UKFI), was established to manage Northern Rock and Bradford & Bingley. In February 2009 a permanent Special Resolution Regime was established. The Treasury acquired majority ownership stakes in both RBS and Lloyds.

Several major European banks also floundered at the height of the financial crisis, during the days and weeks following the September 2008 collapse of Lehman. Hypo Real Estate (HRE), a holding company comprising a number of specialist property finance banks including the troubled Depfa Bank (a German bank headquartered in Dublin which specialized in financing infrastructure projects), was the most prominent German casualty. In October 2008 an initial €50bn rescue package was agreed, comprising a €20bn credit line from the Bundesbank and €30bn of support from other German banks. HRE was subsequently nationalized by the German government and restructured, in one of the largest public bailouts of the global financial crisis.

In September 2008 the share price of Fortis Holdings, a financial services conglomerate based in Belgium, the Netherlands, and Luxembourg, plummeted amid rumours of difficulties in raising short-term funding. In October the Dutch government announced the €16.8bn acquisition of Fortis' Dutch banking and insurance subsidiaries, as well as Fortis' share of ABN AMRO's retail business. The sale of a 75 per cent stake in Fortis Bank to BNP Paribas was approved in April 2009. The governments of Belgium, Luxembourg, and France contributed to a joint €6.4bn recapitalization of the Dexia Group, announced at the end of September 2008. The Belgian government also provided guarantees for new borrowing by Dexia, and a capital injection of €1.5bn for the insurance company Ethias. In October ING Group accepted a €10bn Dutch government recapitalization injection. The Dutch government provided smaller capital injections to Aegon (€3bn) and SNS Reaal (€750m).

Throughout the rest of 2008 and 2009, the health of many European banks remained precarious, as did the finances of several governments which, in addition to funding large fiscal deficits accumulated during the 2000s, faced further shortfalls arising, in part, from debts incurred in bailing out distressed banks. Before the financial crisis, investors had assumed that all Eurozone member governments would honour all euro-denominated public debt, implying that the risk of default was negligible on any government bond, regardless of the country of origin. During the crisis, as it became clear that public debt had risen to unsustainable levels in several Eurozone countries, the markets started to factor a non-negligible default risk into the pricing of bonds issued by different Eurozone governments. It was also made clear that the ECB would not act in the same manner as other central banks, as a 'purchaser of last resort' of government debt. Bond yields began to diverge sharply from early 2010, in accordance with the markets' assessment of the default risk for each country. Default would imply withdrawal from euro membership. Borrowing costs spiralled for the governments of countries deemed to be at the highest risk, placing their finances under further strain.

One of the key lessons of the sovereign debt crisis has been the symbiotic nature of the links between the balance sheets of banks and governments. On the one hand, governments have on many occasions ridden to the rescue of distressed banks; and bank bailouts have imposed strains on the public finances. On the other hand, banks hold sizeable portfolios of government debt. As soon as investors start to doubt the creditworthiness of governments, bank balance sheets deteriorate as government bonds are written down in value. If the banks rein in their lending to consumers or business, in an effort to address the deterioration in their balance sheets, there are adverse macroeconomic consequences through reduced spending on consumption and investment, and slow growth. Poor macroeconomic performance places the public finances under further strain, leading to heightened concerns over the risk of default on government debt. If property prices fall, the balance sheets of banks with assets linked to property (mortgages, or MBS) are likely to deteriorate further. The downward spiral becomes self-perpetuating and difficult to escape.

By the end of 2014, five Eurozone member countries, Ireland, Greece, Spain, Portugal, and Cyprus, had been recipients of bailout loans provided by the EU and the International Monetary Fund (IMF), conditional on the implementation of tough austerity measures. The European Financial Stability Facility (EFSF), an SPV established to act as the main vehicle for coordinating bailouts, was established by the twenty-seven EU member states in 2010, to be funded by the Eurozone member states, with authorization to borrow up to €440bn to support guarantees offered to each Eurozone member. The EFSF was enlarged in 2011 to support guarantees of up to €780bn. In 2012 the European Commission outlined proposals to establish a European Banking Union (EBU), with the aim of decoupling sovereign risk from bank risk (see Chapter 8).

Rapid economic growth in Ireland before 2006 coincided with a housing and commercial property market boom, with much of the bank lending for property development financed in the interbank markets. After the property bubble burst in 2007 and interbank lending dried up in 2008, the Irish banks' liquidity and solvency came under severe strain. In September 2008 coverage under the Irish deposit guarantee scheme was raised from 90 per cent to 100 per cent of each individual's deposit, subject to a limit that was increased from €20,000 to €100,000. In October the guarantee was extended to all deposits and some debt categories of the three major domestic banks, Bank of Ireland, Allied Irish Banks (AIB), and Anglo Irish Bank, and three other domestic banks. In January 2009 the nationalization was announced of the third-largest bank, Anglo Irish Bank, amid allegations of inappropriate or fraudulent accounting practices involving the concealment of loans from shareholders. In February the government announced a €7bn recapitalization package for Bank of Ireland and AIB. In return for capital injections of €3.5bn each, the government received preference shares and an option to purchase 25 per cent of the ordinary shares of each bank.

Shortly before the expiry of the blanket guarantee in September 2010, the covered banks were committed to redeeming a large tranche of bonds with maturities that had been aligned with the term of the guarantee. The banks were obliged to borrow from the ECB to cover the bond redemptions. Irish government bond yields climbed to 7 per cent in October, rendering the cost of further market borrowing prohibitive. In November 2010 the Irish government negotiated an €85bn bailout package, which included funding from the EFSF, the IMF, and bilateral loans from other European countries. The Irish government committed to a four-year austerity package, including restraints on public spending and tax rises. In July 2011 the state-owned Anglo Irish Bank was merged with the Irish Nationwide Building Society, which had been taken into state ownership in August 2010, and renamed the Irish Bank Resolution Corporation (IBRC). IBRC was liquidated in 2013. In December 2013 Ireland announced its departure from the bailout programme, after having fulfilled its conditions.

Greece experienced reported growth in GDP averaging 4 per cent per annum over the period 2000–9, driven by a combination of banking sector deregulation, low interest rates, and high government expenditure. However, fast growth, together with flawed and deficient accounting data, masked severe underlying economic problems, including a lack of competitiveness evidenced by declining exports, low labour productivity, and widespread tax evasion and alleged corruption. These problems were manifest in large current account deficits (value of imports exceeds value of exports), large budget deficits (government expenditure exceeds tax revenue), and consequently high levels of government borrowing and debt. Real GDP fell by 0.4 per cent in 2008, and a further 5.4 per cent in 2009. By the end of 2009 the budget deficit as a percentage of GDP stood at 15.2 per cent, and crisis of confidence in the ability of the Greek government to fulfil its sovereign debt obligations triggered a sharp increase in yields on government bonds and a hike in the cost of insurance against default using CDS. Greek banks carried heavy exposures in Greek government bonds, and declining confidence in the solvency of the banks triggered large and sustained outflows of bank deposits.

In May 2010 the Troika, comprising the European Commission, the ECB, and the IMF acting jointly in their capacity as international lenders, sanctioned a €110bn loan to avert the prospect of default on Greek sovereign debt and cover the Greek government's funding requirements until mid-2013. A second package that would eventually amount to €130bn to the end of 2014, including funds for the recapitalization of Greek banks, was announced in 2011 and ratified in February 2012. Under the terms of the second bailout, private sector investors were required to accept extended maturities, reduced interest, and write-offs of 53.5 per cent of the notional value of Greek government bonds. The Greek government agreed to implement tough austerity measures. A €48.2bn bank recapitalization was completed in June 2013, including €24.4bn injected into the four largest Greek banks, NBG, Alpha, Piraeus, and Eurobank.

Between 2010 and 2014 some progress was made towards the reform of the Greek tax system, and there were several privatizations and some labour-market reforms. By the end of 2013 the government deficit had fallen to 3.2 per cent of GDP. In May 2014 a second round of recapitalization for six Greek banks (the big four, plus Attica and Panellinia), amounting to €8.3bn, was privately financed. Such gains, however, were achieved at a heavy cost. Recession was exceptionally severe, with further reductions in real GDP of 5.4 per cent in 2010, 8.9 per cent in 2011, 6.6 per cent in 2012, and 3.3 per cent in 2013, before modest growth of 0.8 per cent returned in 2014. The possibility that Greek politicians or the public would refuse to accept the austerity measures demanded as conditions for bailout funds, resulting in default on Greek sovereign debt and an enforced Greek withdrawal from the euro (Grexit), was a recurring concern throughout the Eurozone crisis. Grexit and the devaluation implied by the creation of a new currency would entail a huge drop in living standards in Greece. Elsewhere a dangerous precedent would be set for other countries, such as Spain, Portugal, and Italy, that could lead to the disintegration of the Eurozone.

Events culminating in the third Greek bailout began with the election of a new coalition government led by the left-wing Syriza party in January 2015, on an anti-austerity platform. Eurozone finance ministers agreed a four-month loan extension in February; but when the extension expired at the end of June Greece fell into arrears with the IMF. After several months of fractious negotiations over a third bailout, the government announced a referendum on the terms proposed by the Troika, and recommended a 'no' vote. On 28 June, during the run-up to the referendum, the Greek banks were closed, ATM withdrawals were subjected to a €60 daily limit, and capital controls (restrictions on the transfer of funds abroad) were imposed. In July the Greek electorate rejected the bailout terms, with a 'no' vote of more than 61 per cent. Faced with the likely alternative of Grexit, however, the Greek government subsequently accepted a third bailout, amounting to $85bn, on terms similar to those rejected in the referendum. The banks reopened on 20 July, and repayments to the IMF and ECB were made, but capital controls remained in force.

Spain has the EU's fifth-largest banking industry. There is a diverse range of ownership types, including commercial banks, savings banks, and specialized credit institutions. Banco Santander and BBVA are large commercial banks with extensive operations in Europe and Latin America. Initially, during 2007 and 2008, the largest Spanish banks wrote off relatively small proportions of their loans portfolios. Two distinctive features of the Bank of Spain's regulatory approach before the crisis have attracted attention. The first was a dynamic provisioning regime, requiring banks to harmonize loan-loss provisioning with the lending cycle, and achieve an accurate accounting recognition of credit risk. Under dynamic provisioning, a loan-loss provision is created at the inception of the loan, reducing the cyclical impact of provisioning. The second aspect is the requirement that assets channelled through Structured Investment Vehicles (SIV) are subject to the same capital requirements as on-balance sheet assets. As a consequence, most Spanish banks abstained from creating off-balance sheet vehicles.

A sharp downturn in the Spanish economy in 2008 was triggered by a property market collapse. The construction industry was decimated, and the rate of unemployment soared from 8.3 per cent in 2007 to 21.6 per cent in 2011. Spanish banks attempted to stave off losses from real-estate lending by acquiring properties from developers, and accumulated large portfolios of empty properties. Unlisted regional savings banks (*cajas*), some of which operated as development banks controlled by regional politicians as well as depositors, were badly affected. Between 2009 and 2012 the number of savings banks was reduced from forty-five to eleven, through a series of emergency mergers and nationalizations. Seven regional savings banks were merged in December 2010 to form the third-largest bank in Spain, Bankia, with Spanish government support.

In June 2012 the Spanish government requested external financial assistance from the EFSF. European Stability Mechanism (ESM) funding of up to €100bn for a period of eighteen months was provided to recapitalize, restructure, and resolve weak banks, allowing for the segregation of the toxic assets of banks requiring public support in an asset-management company. Spain exited the programme in January 2014.

Banks dominate the financial sector in Portugal. Many banks are highly diversified, into insurance, securities, and other non-banking activities. Conservative lending practices and the absence of any real-estate boom limited the exposures of Portuguese banks during the first phase of the financial crisis. Nevertheless, the Portuguese government set up a €20bn loan guarantee fund in October 2008, and in December 2008 announced the availability of up to €5bn for bank recapitalization. Banco Português de Negócios, (BPN) was nationalized by the Portuguese Government after accounting and fraudulent activities were uncovered. A government budget deficit of 9.8 per cent of GDP in 2010, combined with deteriorating macroeconomic conditions and credit-rating downgrades, led to a request for EU and IMF assistance in April 2011. A €78bn programme was offered, conditional on the Portuguese government pursuing austerity measures. The government would stabilize the banking industry by recapitalizing the nation's banks. During 2014 Portugal exited from its three-year adjustment programme on schedule, with the budget deficit targeted to fall to 4 per cent of GDP in 2014 and below 3 per cent in 2015. The collapse of Banco Espírito Santo in July 2014 provided an unwelcome reminder of the difficulties that had sparked the debt crisis.

After joining the EU in 2004 and adopting the euro in 2008, Cyprus became an international banking centre. Low corporate tax rates encouraged an influx of foreign deposits and rapid banking sector growth. Bank regulation and supervision were poorly coordinated, and disagreements between the central bank and Ministry of Finance were commonplace. Cypriot banks attracted large volumes of deposits from Greece and Russia, and held substantial portfolios of Greek government bonds. Real-estate lending contributed to a property market boom, and the banks' balance sheets became dangerously over extended. The bursting of the property market bubble, together with a €4.5bn write-down of Greek government bonds under the terms of the second Greek bailout, caused major difficulties for Cypriot banks in funding their commitments. In May 2012 the Cypriot government rescued Cyprus Popular Bank by granting a €1.8bn loan.

The Cypriot government turned initially to Russia, rather than the EU and the IMF, for emergency support. In early 2011 it sought and received a €2.5bn loan from Russia. Faced with ongoing difficulties, however, in June 2012 the Cypriot government requested assistance from the EU and the IMF to stabilize its financial system and finance its budget deficit. A programme of assistance was agreed by the Troika in March 2013. The programme, which made Cyprus the fifth Eurozone member state to be bailed out, comprises funding of up to €10bn for the period 2013–16.

In a key departure from the terms and conditions of previous Eurozone bailouts, the Cypriot government agreed to merge Cyprus Popular Bank into the Bank of Cyprus, and force the holders of uninsured deposits of more than €100,000 in both banks to absorb losses or convert a portion of their uninsured deposits into capital or equity in the merged bank, allowing the latter to recapitalize. This so-called 'bail-in' was highly controversial and damaged confidence in the banks, necessitating the imposition of temporary controls on domestic and international capital movements in March 2013. Domestic capital controls, which restricted bank withdrawals to a maximum of €300 per day, were eventually lifted in May 2014.

Although the 'bail-in' of uninsured depositors in Cypriot banks shielded EU taxpayers from the costs of yet another rescue package, it may also have increased the likelihood that in any future banking crisis large depositors will take flight rapidly at the first signs of trouble, heightening the risk that more banks will collapse. At the time of writing (mid-2016), the increasing threat of an Italian banking crisis appeared likely to provide a stern challenge to the principle of 'bail-in' of creditors. Against a macroeconomic background of sluggish economic growth, high unemployment, and high levels of public debt, Italian banks were burdened with large volumes of underperforming loans. Many Italian retail investors held bonds issued by Italian banks, making it difficult politically to impose losses on bondholders before banks can be bailed out by the Italian government, as Eurozone rules require.

Chapter 8
Policy and regulatory responses to the global financial crisis

The 2007–9 global financial crisis brought a number of specific policy and regulatory challenges into sharp focus. From an historical perspective, the regulatory response follows a long-established pattern, whereby stricter regulation and supervision is enacted in response to a financial crisis, while pressure leading to financial deregulation tends to mount during times of prosperity, as the previous crisis recedes into history and the collective memory fades.

Evolution of monetary policy

In the area of monetary policy, the earliest adoption of quantitative easing (QE) is attributed to the Bank of Japan, which sought to combat domestic deflation in the early 2000s by purchasing treasury securities and, later, asset-backed securities and corporate bonds, on a scale beyond that required to reduce the interest rate to zero. Purchases equivalent to $300bn in value were completed between 2001 and 2005. In the US, the Federal Reserve sold treasury bills and purchased less liquid assets on a large scale for several months prior to the Lehman collapse, in an effort to pump liquidity into the financial system. This policy has been interpreted as a forerunner of QE, which commenced officially in November 2008. The programme retrospectively known as QE1 involved the purchase by the Federal Reserve of bonds and mortgage-backed securities (MBS) to the value of $600bn that had been issued by the government-sponsored enterprises (GSE) Fannie Mae and Freddie Mac. QE1 was subsequently extended to include the purchase of a further $750bn of GSE securities, and $300bn of US Treasury securities. Purchases under QE1 were completed in March 2010.

Between December 2010 and June 2011, the Federal Reserve purchased $600bn of government bonds with long maturities under QE2. Operation Twist, announced in September 2011, was a credit easing programme for the sale of shorter-dated securities (maturities less than three years) and purchase of longer-dated securities (maturities between six and thirty years). Initially the Federal Reserve committed to purchases and sales to the value of $400bn; a further $267bn was added prior to the end of 2012. In September 2012 the Federal Reserve announced QE3, involving monthly purchases of GSE bonds and MBS to the value of $40bn per month. QE3 was expanded to include purchases of an additional $45bn of government bonds per month, from December 2012. In December 2013 the Federal Reserve announced the scaling back of these sales; QE3 was terminated in October 2014. At its meeting in the same month the Federal Open Market Committee (FOMC) issued forward guidance by affirming that a target range for the federal funds rate of 0 per cent to ¼ per cent is likely to remain appropriate 'for a considerable time' in pursuit of maximum employment and 2 per cent inflation.

In the UK, QE commenced with the purchase by the Bank of England of around £200bn of assets between March 2009 and January 2010: predominantly medium- and long-dated government bonds, and some corporate bonds. Further asset purchases were announced in October 2011 (£75bn), February 2012 (£50bn), and July 2012 (£50bn), bringing the total to around £375bn. In August 2013 the Monetary Policy Committee chaired by Mark Carney, the new Governor, issued a forward guidance statement indicating that the interbank rate would remain 0.5 per cent, and the stock of assets purchased under QE would be maintained at its current level, at least until the rate of unemployment rate had fallen to 7 per cent. In February 2014, following a faster-than-expected fall in unemployment and continued sluggish economic growth, the guidance was modified to refer to a range of indicators, and not solely the unemployment rate.

Critics have argued that QE is tantamount to 'printing money' by electronic means, in the sense that the accounts of the commercial banks selling the securities are credited by the central bank with new reserves created electronically. The extent to which QE feeds through into an inflationary expansion of the money supply depends on the willingness of the banks use the newly created reserves to support additional lending. In the wake of the global financial crisis, many banks were reluctant to lend, and a large proportion of the reserves created by QE either remained on deposit with the central banks, or were channelled into speculative investments in shares, property, or commodities by banks in search of higher yields on their assets. The accumulation of the banks' reserves does not necessarily defuse the inflationary potential of QE, because reserves in existence today can still be used to support increased lending tomorrow. In practice, however, policymakers have been more concerned with the possible deflationary effects of the cessation of QE, than the risk of inflation.

The potentially damaging inflationary consequences of QE may not have materialized, but were QE programmes successful in stimulating economic activity? The contribution of expansionary monetary policy towards recovery has been blunted by the simultaneous adoption of contractionary fiscal policies, by governments preoccupied with reducing budget deficits and public debt. Nevertheless there is a broad consensus that the impact of the global financial crisis would have been more severe in the US and UK had the central banks not intervened in the aggressive manner they did.

In the Eurozone the adoption of QE was resisted until 2015, despite sluggish growth and consistent undershooting of the ECB's 2 per cent inflation target. Germany argued that it would bear a disproportionate share of the costs of any QE programme, and questioned the legality of the purchase of government bonds on the grounds that the ECB is banned from financing governments directly by acquiring sovereign debt. Despite this prohibition, the ECB was active throughout the sovereign debt crisis in purchasing bonds in secondary markets (markets for the trading of bonds already issued). Between 2010 and 2012 the ECB focused on purchases of bonds issued by Eurozone governments, offsetting the additional liquidity that would have been created by accepting additional deposits of funds from the banks equivalent in value to the securities purchased. In 2011 the ECB announced a new programme of low-interest longer-term lending direct to banks, under the Long Term Refinancing Operation (LTRO), designed to supplement the ECB's regular Main Refinancing Operations (MRO) which supply short-term liquidity to banks. Further LTRO bond purchases were announced in 2012 and 2014.

The ECB's QE programme, announced in January 2015, involved bond purchases of €60bn per month between March 2015 and September 2016. Bond yields immediately fell, making it easier for governments to service or pay down their debt, and the capitalization of banks was strengthened through increases in the value of their existing portfolios of bonds held as investments.

An important development since mid-2014 has been the introduction of negative policy interest rates in several countries, implemented through either the imposition of a charge on the banks' reserves (deposits) at the central bank, or the introduction of a negative target for the key policy interest rate. A negative central bank deposit rate should increase the incentives for banks to lend, rather than accumulate reserves at the central bank, thereby boosting the level of economic activity. By discouraging inflows of short-term deposits from foreign investors, a negative interest rate should also help lower the exchange rate, providing a boost to domestically produced exports. By 2016, the 'negative interest club' included the Eurozone, Denmark, Sweden, Switzerland, and Japan, but excluded the US and the UK. The latter two countries may need to maintain higher interest rates to attract investor funds from abroad, in order to finance large current account deficits (trade in goods and services and other flows of income). By contrast several of the countries with negative rates run current account surpluses, and have less pressing need for external finance.

Until recently, many economists would have doubted whether a negative policy interest rate was sustainable, in the belief that depositors (whether banks depositing reserves at the central bank, or customers depositing savings with a retail bank) would rapidly switch to cash in order to avoid depletion of funds on deposit at a negative rate. As well as the possibility of bank runs, there were concerns that negative rates would cause other distortions in economic behaviour. For example, debtors would always prefer to pay early while creditors would sooner be paid late, contrary to the received wisdom. Consumers might attempt to store wealth in the form of gift vouchers or pre-payment cards for travel or mobile phone services. In practice, banks in the countries with negative central bank deposit rates have generally been willing to continue to maintain reserves with the central bank and accept a squeeze on profits, rather than bear the storage, insurance, and transport costs of holding large amounts of cash in their own vaults. Retail depositors have been shielded from negative deposit rates by the banks' concern that negative rates could trigger a run on deposits. The reluctance of banks to impose negative interest rates on deposits, however, has resulted in a squeeze on the banks' profitability.

Recent developments in bank regulation

History suggests that no system of regulatory arrangements is capable of providing a cast-iron guarantee of financial stability. Regulation often tends to be backward-looking, informed by the experience of the previous crisis. At the height of a crisis, supervisors may put off taking tough action to prompt the closure of a distressed bank. Rescue may be the safer option for supervisors or politicians, fearful that collapse could have consequences for financial stability that are hard to foresee. Often, regulators and supervisors are themselves industry insiders, who have worked in the industry previously or hope to do so in the future. Bank executive salaries tend to be higher than those of employees of publicly-funded regulatory agencies. Accordingly, regulated banks may exert undue influence over regulators, a problem known as 'regulatory capture'.

Since the crisis much of the impetus for strengthening the regulatory framework and improving international coordination has come from the Financial Stability Board (FSB) at the Bank for International Settlements (BIS). The FSB comprises senior representatives from ministries of finance, central banks, and supervisory and regulatory authorities of the G20 countries, plus Hong Kong, Singapore, Spain, and Switzerland, as well as international bodies including the ECB and European Commission. The FSB acts as a coordinating body to set policies and minimum standards that its members commit to implement at national level.

The post-crisis arrangements for the capital regulation of banks, devised by the FSB and known as Basel III, modify and extend the three-pillar approach to capital regulation introduced under Basel II (see Chapter 5). New capital and liquidity standards are being phased in between 2013 and 2019. Banks are required to achieve a minimum Solvency Ratio of 7 per cent by 2019, defined as the ratio of shareholder capital to risk-weighted assets. The minimum

Solvency Ratio requirement includes a new 'capital conservation buffer' of 2.5 per cent of risk-weighted assets, intended to strengthen loss-absorbing capacity. In addition, national regulators are permitted to impose a discretionary 'countercyclical capital buffer' of up to 2.5 per cent of risk-weighted assets. The ratio of Tier 1 Capital (shareholder capital plus reserves, or retained earnings) to risk-weighted assets must be at least 6 per cent. Systemically Important Financial Institutions (SIFIs) must hold additional capital in the range 1 per cent to 2.5 per cent. SIFIs are large, interconnected, and complex entities whose failure would disrupt not only the wider financial system, but also investment, employment, and growth in the real economy. Basel III introduced a new Leverage Ratio, requiring banks to maintain a ratio of Tier 1 Capital to total (not risk-weighted) assets of 3 per cent. Banks must maintain a new Liquidity Coverage Ratio (LCR) to ensure they hold sufficient liquid assets to survive a 30-day stress test; and a Net Stable Funding Ratio (NSFR) to limit reliance on short-term wholesale funding.

During the global financial crisis, the issue of too-big-to-fail (TBTF) (see Chapter 5) re-emerged with a vengeance in the debate surrounding the controversial bailout of Bear Stearns, and the equally controversial decision *not* to rescue Lehman Brothers. During this phase, it was suggested that a more relevant criterion for identifying institutions that could not be permitted to fail under any circumstances was their degree of interconnectedness with other financial or non-financial institutions. The term too-interconnected-to-fail (TITF) has been coined to capture the notion that, although size and interconnectedness may be correlated they are not synonymous; and the interconnectedness of a distressed bank is the key determinant of the level of systemic risk its failure would pose.

Interconnectedness creates problems when banks are excessively reliant on each other for short-term funding. If one bank withdraws temporarily from lending to other banks, interbank lending markets can rapidly seize up, jeopardizing the stability of banks generally and the financial system. Another example of interconnectedness concerns a bank that has entered into large numbers of credit default swap (CDS) or other derivatives contracts, with other financial institutions as counterparties. In the event that the bank fails, these contracts would not be honoured, and the default would carry the potential to jeopardize the stability of the counterparties.

Bank levies have been introduced in many developed countries, especially in Europe. These taxes act as a complement to other forms of prudential regulation. One objective is to impose a larger proportion of the costs of implicit guarantees and taxpayer-funded bailouts on the banks themselves. Typically, bank levies are charged on bank liabilities such as deposits; the specific types of liability subject to the levy vary between countries. Some countries, including the Netherlands and the UK, have introduced progressive scales, which impose most or all of the burden on the larger banks. In the UK, a phased reduction in the bank levy will be offset by a tax surcharge on profits, operative from 2016. Tax revenues raised from bank levies may be directed into specific bank resolution funds (as in Germany), or added to general tax revenue (as in the UK). There is some evidence that banks have shifted much of the additional tax burden on to customers, by increasing the rates charged on loans to borrowers, and reducing the rates paid to savers.

The global financial crisis strengthened the case for the introduction (or reintroduction) of separation between commercial and investment banking, as operated in the US between 1933 and 1999. The objective would be to isolate retail banking from possible losses arising from speculative investment banking trading. Paul Volcker, a former US Federal Reserve Chairman, argued that the banks' involvement in derivatives trading had contributed to excessive systemic risk prior to the crisis. The so-called Volcker rule, incorporated into the Dodd–Frank Act of 2010, prohibits US banks, or any institution that owns a bank, from engaging in proprietary trading in securities, derivatives, commodity futures, and options on their own account. Such trading on behalf of clients is still permitted. Full compliance with the Volcker rule was required by July 2015. Critics have argued that the ability to trade in securities is an essential tool in risk management, and the rule fails to discriminate between trading activities that reduce risk, such as hedging, and purely speculative trading. Trading in securities on behalf of clients and proprietary trading may be hard to distinguish in practice. When lobbying against the rule, the banks argued that their international competitiveness would be damaged by restrictions on their permissible activities.

In the UK the Independent Commission on Banking, chaired by John Vickers, recommended in 2011 that banks should ring-fence their retail banking divisions from their trading or investment banking operations. Banks with deposits of more than £25bn will be required to place their retail operations and trading operations into separate subsidiaries from 2019. The entities on both sides of the ring-fence will need to demonstrate that they could operate independently, and the retail entity will be subject to more stringent capital requirements. Banks will be allowed leeway to design their own business models, and will be required to demonstrate compliance.

For Europe, the 2012 Liikanen Committee report offered a further variation on ring-fencing, in proposals that had not been written into legislation at the time of writing. Liikanen, the governor of the Bank of Finland, proposed that banks with more than €100bn in assets used to support trading, or for which such assets represent at least 15 per cent to 25 per cent of total assets, should place their trading activities into a trading bank constituted as a separate legal entity. The trading bank would not be funded from retail deposits, and would not offer retail payment services. Retail banks would continue to use derivatives for risk-management and hedging, and both entities must independently satisfy capital requirements.

Micro-prudential regulation refers to regulatory measures targeted at individual banks, while macro-prudential regulation involves measures aimed at enhancing the stability of the financial system as a whole. Macro-prudential regulation and supervision is designed to address systemic risk, created by interconnectedness, or interactions between banks and other financial and non-financial institutions. Since the global financial crisis the FSB has identified twenty-eight Global Systemically Important Banks (G-SIBs) based on their size, interconnectedness, and complexity according to qualitative judgement. Sixteen of these banks are headquartered in Europe, eight in the US, three in Japan, and one in China. It is proposed that G-SIBs should be subject to more intrusive supervision than other banks, and hold additional capital in proportion to the estimated broad economic costs that would arise from failure. In November 2014 the FSB announced proposals for G-SIBs to be required to demonstrate a loss-absorbing capacity equivalent to 16–20 per cent of total assets.

Bankers' pay and bonuses have been subject to intense public scrutiny since the financial crisis. The amounts paid in bonuses by the large banks to their own employees are substantial. According to figures for the UK quoted by the *Guardian*, in 2012 HSBC's profits were £7bn and its bonus pool was £1.8bn; 204 HSBC employees worldwide were each paid more than £1m. Barclays' profits were £13.7bn, and its bonus pool was £2.4bn, with 428 employees paid more than £1m. RBS, despite reporting losses of £5bn, created a bonus pool of £607m; and Lloyds, with losses of £5m, created a bonus pool of £375m. Bonus payments to the senior executives of banks such as RBS and Lloyds that had been bailed out using taxpayer funds proved especially toxic for the banks' own public relations, and for governing politicians. In 2012 Fred Goodwin, a former CEO of RBS, was stripped of a knighthood awarded in 2004 for services to the banking industry.

Despite public anger, politicians have shown reluctance to legislate on executive compensation, preferring to leave remuneration as a matter for market forces to shape and boards of directors to decide. As with any regulation with less-than-universal geographical coverage, it has been argued that the market for executive talent is global, and restrictions imposed in one region would simply encourage executives or banks themselves to relocate to jurisdictions without restrictions. One notable exception is the EU, which introduced legislation in 2014 to cap bonuses at 100 per cent of salary, unless at least 65 per cent of shareholders (75 per cent if there is no quorum) approve an increase to 200 per cent. Opponents argue that a cap on bonuses will simply lead to higher salaries, as banks seek to maintain total compensation at equivalent levels. If banks respond by increasing salaries, a higher fixed element in total compensation affords banks less flexibility, rather than more, to adjust costs if trading conditions deteriorate. A tax on bank bonuses, imposed in the UK temporarily in 2009, may have encouraged banks to pay higher gross bonuses in order to preserve net payouts.

The London Interbank Offered Rate (or Libor) is the rate of interest at which banks lend to each other overnight on the London interbank market. Libor is also the rate used as a benchmark for pricing other loans to households, corporations, and governments, as well as many other securities such as derivatives. Until recently rates were calculated for ten currencies over fifteen borrowing periods, ranging from overnight to one year, and published daily. Historically, Libor was overseen by the British Bankers' Association, and based on quotations (not actual rates) submitted by eighteen large banks. Each morning banks submit their estimates of borrowing costs to Thomson Reuters. The highest and lowest 25 per cent of submissions are disregarded and Libor is the average of the remaining submissions.

In 2008 a *Wall Street Journal* article alleged manipulation of Libor rates; and in 2012 substantial further evidence emerged.

During the financial crisis some banks deflated their estimates of Libor, so as to make themselves appear more creditworthy and therefore stronger than they actually were. Many banks stood to earn significant profits on derivatives based on interest rates, if rates were to decline. A series of investigations revealed evidence of widespread manipulation of Libor on several currencies. Several large banks and brokerages, including Barclays, UBS, RBS, Deutsche Bank, and Société Générale, have subsequently paid hefty fines, and in 2015 one former trader was sentenced to lengthy imprisonment. Subsequently the Libor was transferred from the British Bankers' Association to NYSE Euronext Rates Administration (later renamed ICE Benchmark Administration after Intercontinental Exchange (ICE) acquired NYSE Euronext), regulated by the UK's FCA. In July 2014 the FSB announced plans to base benchmark interest rates as much as possible on actual market transactions data, making Libor less susceptible to manipulation. Under a 'twin-track' approach the existing Libor will be strengthened by underpinning using market transactions data; while work commences on developing 'nearly risk-free reference rates' based on market transactions.

Although there is widespread agreement that before the crisis central banks, regulators, and investors were over-reliant on information produced by the credit-rating agencies, progress towards reform in this area has been slow. In the US the Dodd–Frank Act strengthened the regulation of credit-rating agencies; required agencies to disclose how their ratings have performed over time; and required agencies to provide additional information to allow investors to interpret published ratings more effectively. An amendment to the Act specifies that ratings are not protected as free speech, but should be regarded as commercial in character and subject to the same standards of liability and oversight applicable to auditors, securities analysts, and investment bankers. The FSB has called for a reduction in references to agency ratings in standards, laws, and regulations, and for banks and other large investors to disclose information about alternative approaches to credit-risk assessment.

Deficiencies in over-the-counter (OTC) derivatives markets that were exposed during the crisis include a build-up of counterparty risk that was neither adequately recognized nor appropriately managed, and a lack of transparency over the size and concentration of counterparty credit exposures. In 2009 the G20 leaders committed to reforms that would introduce centralized clearing and, where appropriate, electronic trading of standardized OTC derivatives; improved reporting of transactions; and higher capital requirements for non-centrally cleared transactions. In the US the Dodd–Frank Act included provisions for some liquid and standardized derivatives transactions, including CDS, to be subject to central clearing requirements. However, progress towards consistent, timely, and accurate reporting of the data required for regulators to accurately gauge counterparty exposures has been patchy. Several years after the crisis it is doubtful whether regulators' ability to measure the threats posed by derivatives markets for financial stability is much improved.

There is little doubt that the accumulation of risk in the shadow banking system was a factor in the global financial crisis. Since 2011 the FSB has conducted annual monitoring assessments, which have been complemented by exercises carried out by the IMF, the ECB, and regional consultative groups in the Americas and Asia. Several other initiatives to strengthen regulation of the shadow banking system are underway. The FSB tasked the Basel Committee on Banking Supervision (BCBS) with formulating proposals to reduce risks posed by the interaction between traditional banks and shadow banks. New risk-sensitive capital requirements, to be implemented in 2017, are designed to ensure banks hold sufficient capital against investments in the equity of funds (given the underlying investments and leverage of a given fund). A new supervisory framework for measuring and controlling banks' large exposures, to be implemented in 2019, limits the maximum losses a bank might make in the event of the failure of a large counterparty or group of closely interconnected counterparties. The reporting and monitoring of large exposures extends existing capital regulation, and is applicable to all internationally active banks.

The liability structure of money market funds (MMFs) made these funds prone to bank runs during the financial crisis. In October 2012, the International Organization of Securities Commissions, IOSCO (the worldwide association of national securities regulatory commissions) issued final policy recommendations that provide the basis for common standards of regulation and supervision of MMFs. One of the major recommendations is that where possible MMFs should convert to floating, rather than constant, net asset values.

Efforts have been made to improve transparency and align incentives in markets for securitized assets. In November 2012, IOSCO recommended that securitizers should be required to retain a proportion of new securitized issues on their books; and in October 2014 the US authorities adopted a new rule requiring sponsors of asset-backed securities to retain not less than 5 per cent of the credit risk of the underlying assets. In August 2013 the FSB produced a framework for regulatory authorities to assess the systemic risk arising from shadow banking institutions other than MMFs, based upon economic (maturity transformation, liquidity) functions rather than legal form, and a set of policy measures that can be used to reduce risks emanating from the shadow banking sector.

Cross-border banking raises complex issues for supervision and, especially, for resolution in the event of the failure of an international bank that trades in several countries with separate regulatory arrangements. Strains are placed on a supervisory framework organized on national lines, when there is considerable variation between countries in supervisory and regulatory practice. Cooperation between national supervisors is difficult at the best of times, and disputes can delay action in situations where speed is essential. Progress in resolving these issues since the global financial crisis has been patchy.

A cross-border bank's legal structure determines the division of responsibilities between national supervisory authorities. Traditionally the branches of international banks are subject to home-country supervision: in other words, international branches were the responsibility of the supervisor of the country in which the bank was headquartered. By contrast subsidiaries, incorporated as separate legal entities owned by the parent bank, fall within the host-country supervisor's jurisdiction, and so were the responsibility of the supervisor of the country in which the subsidiary was located.

Home-country supervision creates difficulties in the case of failure, if the most immediate and damaging repercussions impact upon the host, rather than the home country. The Icelandic banking collapse of 2008 illustrates the danger of mismatch between the size of a cross-border bank, and the size of a home country's resources available to launch a rescue in the event of failure. Between 2006 and 2008 Landsbanki and Kaupthing set up online banking operations offering high-interest internet accounts to depositors in the UK and the Netherlands in the case of Landsbanki's Icesave brand, and through subsidiaries trading under the Kaupthing Edge brand in nine European countries. When liquidity in the interbank markets dried up in September 2008 following the Lehman collapse, the Central Bank of Iceland had insufficient reserves of euro and sterling to meet the banks' funding requirements as lender of last resort.

In early October Glitnir was placed into receivership; and following a run on savings in Icesave by UK and Dutch online depositors, Landsbanki quickly followed. Since Icesave was a branch (not a subsidiary) of Landsbanki, its UK depositors were not covered by UK deposit insurance; however, the UK government froze Landsbanki's UK assets and announced it would compensate UK retail depositors in full. The UK authorities also placed Kaupthing's UK subsidiary into administration, and sold its internet bank Kaupthing Edge to the Dutch group ING Direct. In Iceland Kaupthing followed into receivership. Relative to the size of its economy—Iceland's population is just over 300,000—the collapse of Iceland's banking system has been adjudged by the IMF as the largest of all time.

Since the global financial crisis, efforts to introduce coordinated international arrangements for the resolution and disposal of assets of failed banks with cross-border operations have made limited progress. The requisite trust in foreign regulators to treat all depositors, creditors, and shareholders even-handedly has not always been forthcoming. Instead, there has been a trend towards what has been described as the fragmentation or 'balkanization' of international banking. The Dodd–Frank Act, for example, requires foreign banks to create separately capitalized intermediate holding companies (IHC), subject to US regulatory oversight, to house any subsidiaries operating in the US. Apart from the costs of achieving compliance with US capital-adequacy requirements in respect of the subsidiary by itself, the establishment of an IHC imposes a host of other costs, including the creation of new management, governance, and reporting frameworks, hiring new employees, and modifying IT systems.

One of the most troublesome issues for large international banks is the need to achieve compliance with multiple rules across different jurisdictions. By creating a complex web of home-country, host-country, and international regulatory constraints, the regulatory authorities may be, either deliberately or inadvertently, addressing the problem of too-big-to-fail (TBTF) through a back-door approach that forces large institutions to downsize. However, this approach may make the financial system less efficient, by effectively precluding the largest banks with the greatest technical expertise from trading internationally.

In June 2012 the European Commission launched proposals to create a European Banking Union (EBU), comprising three pillars.

The first pillar involves a transfer of supervisory responsibilities for 123 banks deemed to be 'significant', from national supervisors to a Single Supervisory Mechanism (SSM) operated by the ECB. The objective is to implement a single harmonized supervisory rulebook based on Basel III, rather than divergent national arrangements. The UK authorities, along with Sweden, have declined to participate in the SSM, which became operational in November 2014.

The second pillar of EBU, a pan-European resolution mechanism, aims to provide for the orderly shutdown of non-viable banks, so minimizing the likelihood of taxpayer-funded bank bailouts. The third pillar is the creation of a European deposit insurance scheme that would operate, alongside the resolution fund, under a common resolution authority. This pillar is controversial, because it implies a form of debt mutualization, whereby deposit protection funded by a member with an orderly banking system would be used to protect depositors in a country with a failing banking system. In addition to those of the EBU, proposals are being developed for a Capital Markets Union (CMU), involving the gradual removal of economic and legal barriers to the integration of European capital markets.

Continued progress towards an EBU and CMU was threatened by the outcome of the UK referendum in June 2016, when voters decided by a narrow majority (51.9% to 48.1%) that the UK should leave (Brexit) the EU. The withdrawal process is triggered when the UK government invokes Article 50 of the Treaty on European Union, initiating a two-year period of negotiation between the UK and the other twenty-seven EU member states to decide future relationships. At the time of writing (mid-2016) a new Prime Minster has been appointed in the UK, and a ministerial post has been created with a specific focus on the terms of withdrawal.

The future structure and location of banking and other financial services, both in the UK and elsewhere, will ultimately depend upon the UK's future relationship with the EU. Prior to Brexit the UK is the largest financial centre in Europe, and London dominates worldwide in areas such as wholesale financial services and trading of major currencies, including the euro. UK banks' access to Europe could be terminated if, upon leaving the EU, the UK loses access to the single market. A UK bank would require a separate licence in every EU member state in which it seeks to trade. A significant portion of banking business could choose to relocate from the UK to other major financial centres in Dublin, Paris, or Frankfurt. Whatever happens, a prolonged period of uncertainty over the terms of Brexit is likely to complicate operational and strategic decision-making at banks currently located in the UK.

Glossary

Adjustable rate mortgage A mortgage with a variable interest rate that is adjusted periodically in line with a defined market rate. The rate may be fixed for an initial period before any adjustments take place.

Adverse selection Occurs when a service is chosen predominantly by a group of buyers who offer a poor return to the seller. For example, borrowers know more about themselves than lenders, and may self-select in such a way that bank loans are taken out predominantly by high-risk borrowers.

Asset-backed commercial paper A short-term security issued by a bank or other financial institution. A company seeking to raise cash sells a stream of expected future revenues to a bank, which in turn sells ABCP to investors. As the revenues are collected by the company, these are passed on via the bank to the investors.

Asset-backed security A security with repayments generated from a pool of underlying assets such as mortgages or student loans. The cash flows emanating from the underlying assets are assigned to tranches bearing different levels of *credit risk*. Investors holding the senior tranches take priority over junior tranche-holders when repayments are made.

Asymmetric information A situation where one party to a transaction has more information than the other party, hindering the smooth functioning of markets. Financial markets are susceptible to asymmetric information problems in the form of *adverse selection* and *moral hazard*.

Broad money A money supply measure, comprising cash held by the non-bank public and commercial banks' *reserves*, and deposits with banks or other financial institutions that can be converted into cash easily.

Capital The difference between a bank's total assets and its liabilities in the form of funds raised from depositors and investors. Capital, also known as equity or net worth, is the shareholders' ownership stake in the bank, providing the bank with a buffer against unanticipated losses.

Collateralized debt obligation A security constructed by repackaging a pool of cash-generating assets into tranches bearing different levels of *credit risk*. The assets might themselves be *asset-backed securities*.

Commercial bank A bank that accepts deposits and extends loans. Commercial banks supply both *retail banking* and *corporate banking* services.

Commercial paper A short-term unsecured security issued by a highly rated financial or non-financial company seeking to raise cash.

Corporate banking The provision of core banking services, including deposit-taking and lending, to large companies.

Corporate bond A fixed-interest security issued by a large company as a means of borrowing.

Credit default swap A *credit derivative*, under which the buyer makes a regular stream of payments to the seller to insure against the possible default of an underlying asset such as a *government bond* or *corporate bond*, or a *mortgage-backed security*. The seller agrees to cover the losses that would arise in the event that the insured asset defaults.

Credit derivative A derivative security which transfers the *credit risk* associated with an underlying asset from one party to another.

Credit easing An unconventional monetary policy pursued by a central bank, involving the purchase of long-term or high-risk securities through *open market operations*, and the sale of short-term or low-risk securities.

Credit rationing A situation when investors cannot obtain funding for viable projects, because banks are unwilling or reluctant to lend.

Credit risk The risk that a borrower or the issuer of a security will fail to meet his obligations to make repayments, causing the bank or security-holder to incur losses.

Credit-rating agency An agency that issues ratings reflecting the riskiness of securities, companies, or countries. Standard and Poor's, Moody's and Fitch IBCA dominate the credit-rating industry.

Currency risk The risk that foreign exchange rate movements cause the balance sheet value of assets to decrease, or the value of liabilities to increase, when banks hold assets and liabilities denominated in different currencies.

Deposit expansion multiplier The (multiple) increase in *broad money* arising from an increase in bank lending in response to an increase in bank deposits.

Deposit insurance A scheme guaranteeing that small depositors are reimbursed (normally to a specific limit) if a bank collapses. Deposit insurance may be funded by banks or by the government.

Deposit rate The interest rate paid by the central bank on deposits placed by commercial banks, known as *reserves*.

Derivative A security whose value is derived from the price of one or more underlying securities or indices.

Discount rate The interest rate charged by a central bank for lending to commercial banks.

Equity See *capital*.

Fire sale An enforced sale of assets at reduced prices, often when a bank encounters a *liquidity* or *capital* shortage.

Forward guidance A verbal commitment on the part of a central bank concerning the future conduct of monetary or interest rate policy.

Forward An *over-the-counter* contract between two parties for the sale and purchase of an asset at a specified price on a specified future date.

Future Similar to *forward*, but purchased and traded on an exchange (rather than *over-the-counter*).

Government bond A fixed-interest security issued by a government as a means of borrowing.

Government-sponsored enterprise In the US, a financial services corporation that facilitates the flow of credit to specific demographic groups or economic sectors. GSEs include the Federal National Mortgage Association (Fannie Mae) and the Federal Home Loan Mortgage Corporation (Freddie Mac), which help low- and medium-income households obtain mortgages.

Interbank market The market for borrowing and lending between banks.

Interest-rate risk The risk that interest rates might increase, obliging a bank to pay higher interest to depositors, while the interest received from loans with non-flexible rates remains unchanged.

Investment bank A bank that provides services to companies, governments, and wealthy private individuals, including assistance in arranging mergers, *underwriting* new security issues, and asset or wealth management. Investment banks also trade in securities, commodities, and derivatives.

Junk bond A *corporate bond* which offers a high return but carries a high *credit risk*.

Lender of last resort Refers to the role of the central bank in providing emergency lending to commercial banks that are temporarily unable to meet their depositors' demands for withdrawals.

Leverage Refers to the amount of debt a bank uses to finance its assets, including investments in securities and lending. Leverage magnifies risk. Borrowing to finance the acquisition of assets may be profitable if the acquired assets deliver returns as expected, but jeopardizes solvency if the assets default.

Liquidity The ease or speed at which an asset can be sold and converted into cash. A liquid asset can be sold easily and quickly.

Liquidity risk The risk that a bank might not hold sufficient liquid assets to be able to meet the demands of its depositors for withdrawal of their funds.

Market risk The risk that a bank's investments in securities might fail to deliver the returns expected, or the securities might fall in value.

Monetary base Cash held by the non-bank public and commercial banks' *reserves*. A narrower money supply measure than *broad money*, also known as narrow money.

Money market fund In the US, a mutual fund which invests in securities such as *commercial paper* and short-term *government bonds*.

Moral hazard A tendency for a person or entity to behave irresponsibly, in the knowledge that someone else will bear the cost of their risky or negligent behaviour. For example, if borrowed funds are not used responsibly, the lender may bear the cost in the event that the borrower defaults.

Mortgage-backed security An *asset-backed security* whose underlying asset is a pool of mortgages.

Narrow money See *monetary base*.

Net worth See *capital*.

Open market operations Purchase or sale by the central bank of securities, such as *government bonds*, with the intention of influencing the money supply.

Operational risk The risk of failure of a bank's physical or human resources, owing to events such as natural disasters, terrorist attacks, or negligence or fraud on the part of employees.

Option A contract which confers the right, but not the obligation, to either buy (call option) or sell (put option) an asset such as a security at a specified price on, or sometimes until, a specified date.

Over-the-counter market A market in which buyers and sellers negotiate and transact directly with each other, without the supervision or mediation of an exchange.

Quantitative easing A central bank policy of purchasing securities from banks and other financial institutions, and supplying *reserves* beyond the quantity required to reduce the target policy interest rate to zero.

Repo The sale of securities, with a commitment by the seller to repurchase at a slightly higher price after a specified period (often overnight). Widely used by banks as a source of short-term funding.

Reserves Highly liquid and secure deposits placed by commercial banks with the central bank.

Retail banking The provision of banking services to consumers, households, and small businesses.

Securitization A practice whereby a bank bundles a large number of loans together, and sells them to a *structured investment vehicle* (SIV). The SIV typically finances its acquisition of the loans by selling *asset-backed securities* or *mortgage-backed securities* to investors, backed by the anticipated future income from the loans.

Settlement risk The risk that one party may fail to meet its financial obligations to another at the time of settlement of a contract.

Shadow banking Refers to financial institutions that offer similar services to banks, but operate without banking licenses and largely beyond the scope of regulation.

Sovereign risk The risk of losses arising from actions taken by a sovereign nation, such as suspension or default on repayments on *government bonds*.

Special purpose vehicle A subsidiary of a financial institution with its own legal status. An SPV may be used by the institution to transfer assets from its own balance sheet, perhaps evading a regulatory requirement to hold capital against the assets concerned.

Stress test An investigation of a bank's capability to absorb losses arising from an unfavourable change in economic conditions, such as an increase in loan defaults or an adverse movement in the market interest rate.

Structured investment vehicle A type of *special purpose vehicle*, which deals in structured securities such as *asset-backed securities* or *mortgage-backed securities*.

Subordinated debt A form of debt which has lower priority, or is subordinate to, other (secured) debt in the queue for repayment in the event that the issuer defaults on its commitments to repay.

Subprime mortgage In the US, a residential mortgage extended to a class of borrower with a low credit rating, or poor credit history.

Swap A *derivative* security which commits the parties to a series of exchanges of cash flows at agreed dates in the future. Common examples are interest rate, currency, and commodity swaps.

Syndicated lending Refers to a large loan made by a group (syndicate) of banks to a large company or government.

Underwriting A commitment on the part of an *investment bank* to purchase any securities from a new issue that are not taken up by investors.

Wholesale banking The provision of financial services to large companies, including both *corporate banking* and *investment banking* services.

Further reading

General

Introductory textbooks covering the theory and practice of banking include *The Economics of Money, Banking and Financial Markets*, 10th edn., by Frederic Mishkin (Pearson, 2012); *Money, Banking and Financial Markets*, 3rd edn., by Stephen Cecchetti and Kermit Schoenholtz (McGraw Hill, 2011); and *Introduction to Banking*, 2nd edn., by Barbara Casu, Claudia Girardone, and Philip Molyneux (Pearson, 2015). At a more technical level, *The Oxford Handbook of Banking*, 2nd edn., edited by Allen Berger, Philip Molyneux, and John Wilson (Oxford University Press, 2015) provides in-depth coverage of banking theory, bank performance, regulation, and macroeconomic themes.

Chapter 1: Origins and function of banking

The articles 'How do Banks Make Money: A Variety of Business Strategies' and 'How Do Banks Make Money? The Fallacy of Fee Income', by Robert DeYoung and Tara Rice (*Federal Reserve Bank of Chicago Economic Perspectives*, 2004, vol. 40) provide an excellent introduction to the functions of banks and sources of bank income. 'The Rise of the Originate-to-Distribute Model and the Role of Banks in Financial Intermediation', by Vitaly Bord and João Santos (*Federal Reserve Bank of New York Economic Policy*

Review, 2012, vol. 18) discusses the transition from financial intermediation to securitized banking. Kushal Balluck, 'Investment Banking: Linkages to the Real Economy and the Financial System' (*Bank of England Quarterly Bulletin*, 2015, quarter 1) describes the functions of investment banks. 'Benchmarking Financial Systems around the World' by Martin Cihák, Asli Demirgüç-Kunt, Erik Feyen, and Ross Levine (*World Bank Policy Research Working Paper*, 2012, no. 6175) describes the development of financial systems around the globe. *Unsettled Account: The Evolution of Banking in the Industrialized World Since 1800*, by Richard Grossman (Princeton University Press, 2010) provides a historical treatment of the evolution of banking since the 1800s. As well as a general overview, the book describes in detail the evolution of banking in England, Sweden, and the United States.

Chapter 2: Financial intermediation

Mark Farag, Damian Harland, and Dan Nixon's 'Bank Capital and Liquidity' (*Bank of England Quarterly Bulletin*, 2013, quarter 3) provides a good introduction to capital and liquidity management. In 'Understanding the Risks Inherent in Shadow Banking: A Primer and Practical Lessons Learned', David Luttrell, Harvey Rosenblum, and Jackson Thies (*Dallas Federal Reserve*, 2012) discuss risk in traditional and shadow banking. The changing nature of financial intermediation, and its role in the global financial crisis, is discussed by Tobias Adrian and Hyun Shin in 'Financial Intermediation and the Financial Crisis of 2007–2009' (*Annual Review of Economics*, 2010, vol. 2).

Chapter 3: Securitized banking

For an introduction to securitization, see Nicola Cetorelli and Stavros Peristiani, 'The Role of Banks in Asset Securitization' (*Federal Reserve Bank of New York Economic Policy Review*, 2012). See also Adrian and Shin cited for Ch. 2. A more detailed and advanced treatment is provided by Gary Gorton in his book *Slapped in the Face by the Invisible Hand: The Panic of 2007* (Oxford University Press, 2010) and his co-authored chapter 'Securitization' with Andrew Metrick, in *The Handbook of the Economics of Finance*, vol. 2, edited by George Constantinides, Milton Harris, and Rene Stulz (Elsevier, 2013).

Chapter 4: The central bank and the conduct of monetary policy

In their article 'Money Creation in the Modern Economy' (*Bank of England Quarterly Bulletin*, 2014, quarter 1), Michael McLeay, Amar Radia, and Ryland Thomas explain the role of commercial banks in the creation of money, and examine recent developments in monetary and interest rate policy, including quantitative easing. Ben Bernanke discusses the changing role of the US Federal Reserve over the past century in his article 'A Century of US Central Banking: Goals, Frameworks, Accountability' (*Journal of Economic Perspectives*, 2013, vol. 27). In 'The Bank of England as a bank' (*Bank of England Quarterly Bulletin*, 2014, quarter 2), Stuart Manning examines the services provided by the Bank of England to the UK government, commercial financial institutions, and other central banks.

Chapter 5: Regulation and supervision of the banking industry

David Llewellyn makes a persuasive case for regulating banks in his paper 'The Economic Rationale for Financial Regulation' (*Financial Services Authority, Occasional Papers Series*, 1999, no. 1). 'The Evolution and Impact of Bank Regulations' (*World Bank Economic Policy Paper* no. 6288, 2012) by James Barth, Gerard Caprio, and Ross Levine, examines the evolution and effectiveness of bank regulation in more than 125 countries. In 'Too Big To Fail: Causes, Consequences, and Policy Responses' (*Annual Review Financial Economics*, 2013, vol. 5), Philip Strahan examines issues of moral hazard in bank regulation. 'Market Discipline in Bank Supervision', by Mark Flannery in *The Oxford Handbook of Banking*, edited by Allen Berger, Phil Molyneux, and John O. S. Wilson (Oxford University Press, 2010) describes how information embodied in bank share and bond prices can be used to improve the supervision of banks.

Chapter 6: Origins of the global financial crisis

In 'Banking Crises: A Review' (*Annual Review of Financial Economics*, 2011, vol. 3), Luc Laeven analyses the causes and consequences of banking crises. Steven Radalet and Jeffrey Sachs survey the Asian financial crisis in 'East Asian Financial Crisis: Diagnosis, Remedies and Prospects' (*Brookings Papers on Economic Activity*, 1998). In 'Dealing with a Banking Crisis: What Can Be Learned from Japan's Experience?' (*Bank of England Quarterly Bulletin*, 2014, quarter 1), Benjamin Nelson examines policy responses to the Japanese banking crisis. John Turner in his book *Banking in Crisis: The Rise and Fall of British Banking Stability, 1800 to the Present* (Cambridge University Press, 2014) details the fortunes of the UK banking industry over two centuries.

Useful sources on the global financial crisis include 'Causes of the Financial Crisis' (*The Economist*, 7 September 2013), *The Bank for International Settlements 2009 Annual Report*, and 'Deciphering the Liquidity and Credit Crunch 2007–08' by Markus Brunnermeier (*Journal of Economic Perspectives*, vol. 23). There are many excellent books on the crisis, including: *The Fall of the House of Credit: What Went Wrong in Banking and What Can Be Done to Repair the Damage?* by Alistair Milne (Cambridge University Press, 2009); *Too Big to Fail: Inside the Battle to Save Wall Street*, by Aaron Sorkin (Allen Lane, 2009); *Fault Lines: How Hidden Fractures Still Threaten the World Economy*, by Raghuram Rajan (Princeton University Press, 2010); *All the Devils Are Here: Unmasking the Men Who Bankrupted the World*, by Joe Nocera and Bethany McClean (Penguin, 2010); *Misunderstanding Financial Crises: Why We Don't See Them Coming*, by Gary Gorton (Oxford University Press, 2012); and *The Shifts and the Shocks: What We've Learned and Have Still to Learn from the Financial Crisis*, by Martin Wolf (Penguin, 2014). Barry Eichengreen's *Hall of Mirrors: The Great Depression, The Great Recession, and the Uses and Misuses of History* (Oxford University Press, 2015) compares the global financial crisis with the Great Depression of the 1930s, while *Fragile by Design: The Political Origins of Banking Crises and Scarce Credit*, by Charles Calomiris and Stephen Haber (Princeton University Press, 2014) examines the politics of financial regulation. In 'Reading about the Financial Crisis: A 21 Book Review' (published in the *Journal of Economic Literature*, 2012, vol. 50), Andrew Lo provides a guide to reading about the crisis. The award-winning documentary *Inside Job*, directed by Charles H. Ferguson, covers the myriad of factors that contributed to the global financial crisis.

Chapter 7: The global financial crisis and the Eurozone sovereign debt crisis

The Euro Trap: On Bursting Bubbles, Budgets, and Beliefs (Oxford University Press, 2014), by Hans Werner-Sinn; and Philip Lane's 'The European Sovereign Debt Crisis' (*Journal of Economic Perspectives*, 2012, vol. 26) describe the sovereign debt crisis in Europe. See also references in further reading for Ch. 6.

Chapter 8: Policy and regulatory responses to the global financial crisis

Alan Blinder's book *After the Music Stopped: The Financial Crisis, The Response, and the Work Ahead* (Penguin, 2013) is a careful account of the policy responses to the financial crisis in the US. For discussion of the tensions between making banks safe while ensuring they continue to lend, see 'Making Banks Safe: Calling to Accounts' (*The Economist*, 5 October 2013). This short article draws on *The Bankers' New Clothes: What's Wrong with Banking and What to Do about It*, by Anat Amdati and Martin Hellwig (Princeton University Press, 2013). See also *The Shifts and the Shocks: What We've Learned and Have Still to Learn from the Financial Crisis*, by Martin Wolf (Penguin, 2014).

For accessible discussions of monetary policy since the crisis, see 'Quantitative Easing', by James Benford, Stuart Rey, Kalin Nikolov, and Chris Young (*Bank of England Quarterly Bulletin*, 2009, quarter 2); 'A Citizen's Guide to Unconventional Monetary Policy', by Renee Haltom and Alexander Wolman (*Federal Reserve Bank of Richmond Economic Brief*, no. 12-12); and 'Monetary Policy after the Crash' (*The Economist*, 27 September 2013). 'Basel III: A Primer. What's New in Banking Risk Regulation?' (*Capgemini*, 2014) describes developments in capital regulation.

John Vickers' chapter, 'Banking Reform in Britain and Europe', in *What Have We Learned? Macroeconomic Policy after the Crisis*, edited by George Akerlof, Olivier Blanchard, David Romer, and Joseph Stiglitz (MIT Press, 2014) provides an overview of banking reforms in the UK and Europe. 'The Dodd–Frank Act: Key Features, Implementation Progress, and Financial System Impact', by James Barth, Penny Prabha, and Clas Wihlborg (Milken Institute, 2015) discusses regulatory change in the US following Dodd–Frank. In 'Dealing with Financial Crises: How Much Help from Research?' (*Centre for Financial Studies Working Paper Series*, no. 481, 2014), Marco Pagano assesses the influence of academic research on policy since the global financial crisis.

Index

ADVERTISING
A Very Short Introduction
Winston Fletcher

The book contains a short history of advertising and an explanation of how the industry works, and how each of the parties (the advertisers , the media and the agencies) are involved. It considers the extensive spectrum of advertisers and their individual needs. It also looks at the financial side of advertising and asks how advertisers know if they have been successful, or whether the money they have spent has in fact been wasted. Fletcher concludes with a discussion about the controversial and unacceptable areas of advertising such as advertising products to children and advertising products such as cigarettes and alcohol. He also discusses the benefits of advertising and what the future may hold for the industry.

www.oup.com/vsi

GLOBALIZATION
A Very Short Introduction
Manfred Steger

'Globalization' has become one of the defining buzzwords of our time - a term that describes a variety of accelerating economic, political, cultural, ideological, and environmental processes that are rapidly altering our experience of the world. It is by its nature a dynamic topic - and this *Very Short Introduction* has been fully updated for 2009, to include developments in global politics, the impact of terrorism, and environmental issues. Presenting globalization in accessible language as a multifaceted process encompassing global, regional, and local aspects of social life, Manfred B. Steger looks at its causes and effects, examines whether it is a new phenomenon, and explores the question of whether, ultimately, globalization is a good or a bad thing.

www.oup.com/vsi

INTERNATIONAL RELATIONS
A Very Short Introduction
Paul Wilkinson

Of undoubtable relevance today, in a post-9-11 world of growing political tension and unease, this *Very Short Introduction* covers the topics essential to an understanding of modern international relations. Paul Wilkinson explains the theories and the practice that underlies the subject, and investigates issues ranging from foreign policy, arms control, and terrorism, to the environment and world poverty. He examines the role of organizations such as the United Nations and the European Union, as well as the influence of ethnic and religious movements and terrorist groups which also play a role in shaping the way states and governments interact. This up-to-date book is required reading for those seeking a new perspective to help untangle and decipher international events.

www.oup.com/vsi

CITIZENSHIP
A Very Short Introduction
Richard Bellamy

Interest in citizenship has never been higher. But what does it mean to be a citizen of a modern, complex community? Why is citizenship important? Can we create citizenship, and can we test for it? In this fascinating Very Short Introduction, Richard Bellamy explores the answers to these questions and more in a clear and accessible way. He approaches the subject from a political perspective, to address the complexities behind the major topical issues. Discussing the main models of citizenship, exploring how ideas of citizenship have changed through time from ancient Greece to the present, and examining notions of rights and democracy, he reveals the irreducibly political nature of citizenship today.

> 'Citizenship is a vast subject for a short introduction, but Richard Bellamy has risen to the challenge with aplomb.'
>
> Mark Garnett, TLS

ECONOMICS
A Very Short Introduction
Partha Dasgupta

Economics has the capacity to offer us deep insights into some of the most formidable problems of life, and offer solutions to them too. Combining a global approach with examples from everyday life, Partha Dasgupta describes the lives of two children who live very different lives in different parts of the world: in the Mid-West USA and in Ethiopia. He compares the obstacles facing them, and the processes that shape their lives, their families, and their futures. He shows how economics uncovers these processes, finds explanations for them, and how it forms policies and solutions.

'An excellent introduction . . . presents mathematical and statistical findings in straightforward prose.'

Financial Times

PRIVACY
A Very Short Introduction
Raymond Wacks

Professor Raymond Wacks is a leading international expert
on privacy. For more than three decades he has published
numerous books and articles on this controversial subject.
Privacy is a fundamental value that is under attack from several
quarters. Electronic surveillance, biometrics, CCTV, ID cards,
RFID codes, online security, the monitoring of employees,
the uses and misuses of DNA, - to name but a few - all raise
fundamental questions about our right to privacy. This *Very Short
Introduction* also analyzes the tension between free speech
and privacy generated by intrusive journalism, photography,
and gratuitous disclosures by the media of the private lives
of celebrities. Professor Wacks concludes this stimulating
introduction by considering the future of privacy in our society.

www.oup.com/vsi

SOCIAL MEDIA
Very Short Introduction

Join our community

www.oup.com/vsi

- Join us online at the official Very Short Introductions **Facebook** page.
- Access the thoughts and musings of our authors with our online **blog**.
- Sign up for our monthly **e-newsletter** to receive information on all new titles publishing that month.
- Browse the full range of Very Short Introductions online.
- Read **extracts** from the Introductions for free.
- If you are a teacher or lecturer you can order inspection copies quickly and simply via our website.

ONLINE CATALOGUE
A Very Short Introduction

Our online catalogue is designed to make it easy to find your
ideal Very Short Introduction. View the entire collection by subject
area, watch author videos, read sample chapters, and download
reading guides.

http://fds.oup.com/www.oup.co.uk/general/vsi/index.html